THE NEW

COOKING

WITH

4

INGREDIENTS

Jean Coates

The New Cooking With 4 Ingredients

1st Printing   January 2002   50,000 copies
2nd Printing   June 2002   30,000 copies

ISBN 1-931294-09-7
Library of Congress Number: 2001099915

Illustrations by Nancy Murphy Griffith

Edited, Designed, Published and Manufactured in the
United States of America by
Cookbook Resources, LLC
541 Doubletree Drive
Highland Village, Texas 75077
972-317-0245

Toll Free Orders: 866/229-2665
www.cookbookresources.com

Preserving the family meal

INTRODUCTION

In our fast-paced, rush-here-and-there lives, a home cooked meal may be considered a luxury. We live out of our cars, placing food orders on cell phones and going to drive-through windows for the nights' meal and maybe the family sits down together to eat.

We want to help families come back to the table and spend quality time while sharing good food to eat. The recipes in "The New Cooking With 4 Ingredients" are easy to prepare and the ingredients are readily available. Most of them are already in your pantry.

Everyone in the family can cook out of "The New Cooking With 4 Ingredients". Mouth-watering meals are just minutes away and every minute we spend around the table enriches our lives and helps us grow stronger.

Please enjoy and don't hesitate to recruit some helpers.

Jean C. Coates

Contents

Contents

APPETIZERS
&
BEVERAGES

Chorizo Cheese Dip

1 (12 ounce) package
  fresh pork chorizo

1 (2 pound) package mild
  Mexican Velveeta

1 (15 ounce) can stewed
  tomatoes

Tortilla chips

- Saute chorizo until cooked; drain.
- In a double boiler, melt the cheese and tomatoes.
- Combine chorizo and cheese mixture, blending well. Serve with tortilla chips.

Speedy Cheese Dip

2 (10½ ounce) cans
  cheddar cheese soup

1 (10½ ounce) can diced
  tomatoes and green
  chilies

1 (10½ ounce) can cream
  of chicken soup

Pinch of cayenne pepper

- Mix all ingredients together in a saucepan (add ½ teaspoon salt to taste). Serve hot. Serve with chips.

Zippy Cheese Dip

1 pound ground beef

½ pound hot pork
  sausage

1 (12 ounce) jar hot salsa

1 (2 pound) box Velveeta
  cheese, cubed

- Brown ground beef and sausage in large skillet, stirring until it crumbles; drain and return to skillet.
- Add salsa and cut up cheese. Cook over low heat, stirring constantly, until cheese melts. Serve warm with chips.

Artichokes and Chips

1 (14 ounce) can artichokes, undrained, quartered

1 ¼ cup grated parmesan cheese

1 (4 ounce) can chopped green chilies, undrained

1 ¼ cup mayonnaise

- Combine all ingredients in blender, mixing well.
- Pour into a greased 9-inch casserole dish.
- Bake at 350° for 25 minutes or until browned around the edges. Serve with chips.

Spicy Beef and Cheese Dip

1 (10 ounce) can tomatoes and green chilies

½ teaspoon garlic powder

1 (2 pound) box Velveeta cheese

1 pound lean ground beef, browned and drained

- In a large saucepan, place tomatoes and green chilies, garlic and cheese, cut in chunks.
- Heat on low until cheese is melted.
- Add the ground beef, mixing well. Serve with tortilla chips.

Crazy Nuts and Cream

2 (8 ounce) packages cream cheese

1 cup sour cream

1 envelope Italian-style dry salad mix

1 cup finely chopped pecans

- Combine first 3 ingredients, beating until blended and smooth.
- Stir in pecans. Chill. Serve with assorted crackers.

Velvet Dip

1 (2 pound) box Mexican
Velveeta cheese, cubed

2 cups mayonnaise

1 (4 ounce) jar chopped
pimentos

1 (7 ounce) can chopped
green chilies

• Place cheese in saucepan and melt over low heat.

• Add other ingredients and mix well. Serve with chips.

Veggie Dip

1 pint sour cream

1 (10 ounce) package
frozen, chopped
spinach, thawed, well
drained

1 package dry vegetable
soup mix

1 bunch fresh green
onions, chopped with
tops

• Combine all ingredients (make sure spinach is well drained).

• Chill for several hours before serving. (Adding ¾ cup chopped pecans would be good in this dip).

Creamy Onion Dip

2 (8 ounce) packages
cream cheese, softened

3 tablespoons lemon
juice

1 package dry onion soup
mix

1 (8 ounce) carton sour
cream

• Beat cream cheese until smooth. Blend in lemon juice and onion soup mix.

• Gradually fold in sour cream until well blended.

• Chill. Serve with chips, crackers or fresh vegetables.

Cold Curry Dip

1½ cups mayonnaise

2 teaspoons curry powder

1 tablespoon grated onion

½ teaspoon dry mustard

- Combine mayonnaise, curry powder, onion and mustard.
- Chill at least 1 hour before serving. Several dashes of Tabasco may be added.

Serve with chilled vegetables such as celery sticks, sliced zucchini or carrot sticks.

Fiesta Onion Dip

1 package dry onion soup mix

1 (15 ounce) can Mexican stewed tomatoes

2 teaspoons chili powder

1 cup grated cheddar cheese

- In small saucepan heat soup mix, tomatoes and chili powder. Bring to a boil.
- Turn heat down and simmer for 20 minutes, stirring occasionally.
- To serve, pour into a serving bowl and sprinkle with the cheese. Stir before serving. Serve with chips.

Broccoli Cheese Dip

1 (10½ ounce) can broccoli cheese soup

1 (10 ounce) package frozen, chopped broccoli, thawed

½ cup sour cream, ½ teaspoon seasoned salt

2 teaspoons of dijon style mustard

- In a saucepan combine soup, broccoli, sour cream, salt and mustard, mixing well. Heat and serve hot.

Hot Broccoli Dip

1 (2 pound) box Mexican Velveeta cheese

1 (10 ounce) can golden mushroom soup

1 (10 ounce) box frozen chopped broccoli, thawed

Chips

- In saucepan, melt cheese with the soup and stir in broccoli.
- Heat thoroughly. Serve with chips. Serve hot.

Broccoli Dip

1 (10 ounce) package frozen, chopped broccoli, thawed

1 (10½ ounce) can cream of chicken soup

3 cups grated cheddar cheese

1 (7 ounce) can chopped green chilies

- In saucepan, cook broccoli about 5 minutes in a little margarine and about ½ teaspoon salt.
- Add soup, cheese and green chilies.
- Heat until cheese melts. (If chilies are not hot enough in the dip, add several dashes of Tabasco). Serve with tostados.

Artichoke Blue Cheese Dip

1 stick butter

1 (14 ounce) can artichoke hearts, drained

1 (4 ounce) package blue cheese

2 teaspoons lemon juice

- In skillet, melt butter and mix in artichoke hearts that have been chopped.
- Add blue cheese and lemon juice. Serve hot.

12

Sassy Onion Dip

1 (8 ounce) package
cream cheese, softened

1 (8 ounce) carton sour
cream

½ cup chili sauce

1 package dry onion soup
mix

• Beat cream cheese until fluffy.
• Add remaining ingredients and mix well.
  Cover and chill. Serve with strips of raw
  zucchini, celery, carrots, etc.

Cottage Dip

1 (16 ounce) carton small
curd cottage cheese

1 envelope dry onion
soup mix

½ cup mayonnaise

½ teaspoon garlic powder

• Blend all ingredients.
• Chill and serve with chips, crackers or
  veggies.

Hot to Trot Dip

1 pound ground beef

1 (2 pound) box Velveeta
cheese, cubed

1½ cups salsa

Several drops of Tabasco

• Brown ground beef and drain well.
• In saucepan, heat cheese and salsa
  until cheese is melted. Add Tabasco.
• Combine meat and cheese mixture.
  Serve hot with tortilla chips.

Five-Minute Dip

1 (8 ounce) package
  cream cheese, softened

1 cup mayonnaise

1 package ranch-style
  salad dressing mix

½ onion, finely minced

- Combine cream cheese and mayonnaise and beat until creamy.
- Stir in salad dressing mix and onion.
- Chill and serve with fresh vegetables.

Horsey Shrimp Dip

1 (6 ounce) can tiny
  shrimp, chopped and
  drained

3 tablespoons creamed-
  style horseradish

⅓ cup mayonnaise

½ teaspoon cajun
  seasoning

- Combine shrimp, horseradish, mayonnaise and seasoning.
- Refrigerate. Serve with crackers.

Sombrero Dip

1 (15 ounce) can chili, no
  beans

½ teaspoon chili powder

¾ cup green chili sauce

1 (2½ ounce) can sliced
  black olives, drained

- Combine chili and chili powder in saucepan. Warm over low heat.
- Stir in sauce and olives. Serve with chips.

Avocados Ole!

3 large ripe avocados, mashed

1 tablespoon fresh lemon juice

1 package dry onion soup mix

1 (8 ounce) carton sour cream

• Mix avocados with lemon juice and blend in soup mix and sour cream. You may want to add a little salt. Serve with chips or crackers.

Tomato Dip

1 (10 ounce) can tomatoes and green chilies, drained

1 (8 ounce) carton sour cream

1½ teaspoons seasoned salt

2 teaspoons horseradish

• Combine all ingredients. Chill. Serve with chips.

Indian Corn Dip

1 pound lean hamburger

½ onion, chopped

1 (15 ounce) can whole kernel corn, drained

1 (12 ounce) jar taco sauce

• Brown hamburger and onion. Add corn, taco sauce and ¼ cup water.

• Simmer mixture for 15 to 20 minutes. Serve with tortilla chips.

Picante and Cream

1 cup sour cream
½ teaspoon prepared
  mustard
½ cup hot picante sauce
½ teaspoon celery salt

• Combine all ingredients.
• Chill. Serve with chips.

Whiz Bang Dip

1 ½ pounds ground beef
¼ cup chopped onion
1 (2 pound) box Mexican
  Velveeta cheese, cubed
¾ cup mayonnaise

• In skillet brown meat and onion, drain.
• Combine all ingredients and mix well.
• On low heat, cook until cheese is melted, stirring constantly. Serve with chips.

Mexican Meat Dip

1 pound lean ground beef
1 pound hot pork sausage
1 (10½ ounce) can golden
  mushroom soup
1 (2 pound) box Mexican
  Velveeta cheese, cubed

• Brown hamburger meat and sausage, drain.
• In separate pan on low heat, combine soup and cheese, blending until smooth.
• Mix with meats and stir thoroughly. Serve with chips.

Whipped Beef Dip

1 (2½ ounce) jar dried beef, coarsely chopped

1 (8 ounce) package shredded cheddar cheese

⅔ cup mayonnaise

½ teaspoon garlic powder

• Combine all ingredients and mix well. (The easiest way to chop dried beef is with scissors). Serve with crackers.

If you would rather serve it hot, spread the mixture on crackers and bake at 350° for about 8 minutes.

Confetti Dip

1 (15 ounce) can whole kernel corn, drained

1 (15 ounce) can black beans, drained

⅓ cup Italian salad dressing

1 (16 ounce) jar salsa

• Combine all ingredients.

• Refrigerate several hours before serving. Serve with chips.

Mustard Dip

1 cup white vinegar

1 (2 ounce) can dry mustard

3 eggs, well beaten

1 cup sugar

• Combine vinegar and mustard; mix well. Refrigerate 24 hours.

• Add eggs and sugar and mix well. Cook on low until thickened.

• Pour into jars and refrigerate. Serve with cocktail sausages or any other food served with mustard.

Dill Deal

1 cup sour cream

1 tablespoon dill, ½
  teaspoon seasoned salt

½ cup mayonnaise

2 tablespoons lemon
  juice

• Combine all ingredients in mixer. Blend at low speed.

• Refrigerate several hours to let flavors blend.

Ham Dip

2 (8 ounce) packages
  cream cheese, softened

2 (6 ounce) cans deviled
  ham

1 heaping tablespoon
  horseradish

¼ cup minced onion

• In mixer, beat cream cheese until creamy.

• Add all other ingredients. Chill and serve with crackers.

Desert Bean Dip

1 (10½ ounce) can
  condensed black bean
  soup, undiluted

2 cups hot picante sauce

1 (8 ounce) carton sour
  cream

1 teaspoon chili powder

• Combine all ingredients and heat in saucepan. Stir to blend flavors. Serve hot with chips.

Veggie Dill Dip

1 cup mayonnaise

2 tablespoons fresh green onions, finely chopped

¼ teaspoon seasoned salt

1 ½ teaspoons dill

- Mix all ingredients and chill. Serve with celery sticks, carrots, cucumber and cherry tomatoes.

Sprinkle a little additional dill, if you like.

Party Shrimp Dip

1 (8 ounce) package cream cheese, softened

½ cup mayonnaise

1 (6 ounce) can tiny, cooked shrimp, drained

¾ teaspoon creole seasoning

- Blend cream cheese and mayonnaise in mixer.
- Stir in shrimp and seasoning.
- Mix well and chill. Serve with chips.

Quick Shrimp Dip

1 (8 ounce) package cream cheese, softened

1 (8 ounce) bottle of cocktail sauce

1 teaspoon Italian seasoning

1 (6 ounce) can tiny, deveined shrimp, drained

- Place cream cheese in mixing bowl and beat until it is smooth.
- Add remaining ingredients and chill. Serve with crackers.

Shrimp Dip

2 (6 ounce) cans shrimp, drained

2 cups mayonnaise

6 green onions, finely chopped

¾ cup chunky salsa

- Crumble shrimp and stir in mayonnaise, onion and salsa.
- Chill for 1 to 2 hours. Serve with crackers.

Tasty Tuna Dip

1 (6 ounce) can tuna in spring water, drained and flaked

1 envelope Italian salad dressing mix

1 (8 ounce) carton sour cream

¼ cup chopped black olives, drained

- Combine all ingredients, stirring until blended.
- Chill 8 hours. Serve with melba rounds.

Cheese Crab Dip

1 (6 ounce) roll processed garlic cheese, diced

1 (10½ ounce) can cream of mushroom soup

1 (6 ounce) can crabmeat, drained

2 tablespoons sherry

- In medium size pan heat all ingredients until cheese has melted.
- Keep warm in a chafing dish and serve with assorted crackers.

Gitty-Up Crab Dip

1 (8 ounce) package
  cream cheese, softened

3 tablespoons salsa

2 tablespoons prepared
  horseradish

1 (6 ounce) can crabmeat,
  drained and flaked

- In mixing bowl, beat cream cheese until creamy.
- Add the salsa and horseradish, mix well.
- Stir in the crabmeat. Refrigerate. Serve with assorted crackers.

Crab Pot Dip

¼ stick margarine

2 cups sharp shredded
  American cheese

⅓ cup dry white wine (or
  cooking wine)

1 (6 ounce) can crab-
  meat, drained

- Melt margarine and cheese, stirring constantly.
- Add wine and crabmeat and heat thoroughly. Serve with crackers.

Hot Crab Dip

2 (8 ounce) packages
  cream cheese, softened

½ cup mayonnaise

2 tablespoons
  worcestershire sauce

1 (6 ounce) can crabmeat,
  drained, flaked

- Beat cream cheese until creamy and add remaining ingredients.
- Pour into a greased 9-inch baking dish.
- Bake at 350° for 15 minutes. Serve with chips or crackers.

Crabmeat Dip

1 (6 ounce) can crabmeat, drained, flaked

1 (8 ounce) package cream cheese, softened

2 (10½ ounce) cans celery soup

1 (4 ounce) can chopped black olives, drained

- In a saucepan combine all ingredients until cheese melts. Serve hot with crackers.

You might also want to add several drops of Tabasco.

Unbelievable Crab Dip

1 (6 ounce) can of white crabmeat, drained, flaked

1 (8 ounce) package cream cheese

1 stick butter

Chips or crackers

- In a saucepan combine crabmeat, cream cheese and butter.
- Heat and mix thoroughly. When mixed, transfer to chafing dish and serve with chips or crackers.

Easy Tuna Dip

1 (6 ounce) can tuna, drained

1 package dry Italian salad mix

1 (8 ounce) carton sour cream

2 green onions with tops, chopped

- Combine all ingredients, mixing well. Let set several hours before serving.

California Clam Dip

1 envelope dry onion
soup mix

2 (8 ounce) carton sour
cream

1 (7 ounce) can minced
clams, drained

2 tablespoons chili sauce

• Combine onion soup mix and sour
cream and mix well. Add clams and
chili sauce. Chill.

Clam Dip

12 ounces cream cheese

½ stick margarine

2 (6 ounce) cans minced
clams, drained

½ teaspoon
worcestershire sauce

• Melt cream cheese and margarine in
double boiler.

• Add drained minced clams and
worcestershire sauce. Serve hot.

Cottage Ham Dip

1 (16 ounce) carton small
curd cottage cheese,
drained

2 (6 ounce) cans deviled
ham

1 package dry onion soup
mix

½ cup sour cream

• Blend cottage cheese in blender or with
mixer.

• Add ham, soup mix and sour cream,
mixing well. Serve with crackers.

Speedy Chili Con Queso

1 (16 ounce) box Velveeta cheese, cubed

½ cup milk

1 (12 ounce) jar salsa

Tortilla chips

- In saucepan, melt the cheese and milk on top of double boiler.
- Add about ½ the salsa. Serve with tortilla chips.

  Taste and add more sauce as needed for desired heat!

Beef Roll

2 (8 ounce) packages cream cheese, softened

½ medium onion, grated

2 tablespoons lemon juice

1 (2 ½ ounce) jar dried beef

- Whip the cream cheese until fluffy. Season with grated onion, lemon juice and a couple dashes of Tabasco.
- Place dried beef on a long roll of wax paper. Spread cream cheese thinly over the beef.
- Roll tightly and refrigerate. Cut into thin slices when ready to serve.

Sausage Balls

1 pound hot pork sausage, uncooked

1 pound grated cheddar cheese

3 cups biscuit mix

⅓ cup milk

- Combine all ingredients and form into small balls. If dough is a little too sticky, add a teaspoon more biscuit mix.
- Bake at 375° for 13 to 15 minutes.

Hot Cheese Balls

1 small jar cheese spread

½ stick margarine, softened

½ cup flour

⅛ teaspoon salt

- Mash cheese spread and the margarine, mixing well. Add flour and salt. Mix well.
- Roll into small balls. Chill one hour.
- Place on ungreased cookie sheet.
- Bake at 425 ° for 10 minutes. Balls will flatten as they cook. Serve hot.

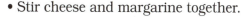

Chili Cheese Balls

1 (8 ounce) package grated sharp cheddar cheese, softened

1 stick margarine, softened

1 cup flour

1 (4 ounce) can chopped green chilies, drained

- Stir cheese and margarine together.
- Add flour, green chilies and ½ teaspoon salt.
- Form dough into 2-inch balls and place on cookie sheet. Bake at 375° for 14 to 15 minutes.

Blue Cheese Ball

3 fresh green onions

1 (8 ounce) and 1 (3 ounce) package cream cheese, softened

1 (4 ounce) package blue cheese, softened

⅓ cup chopped pecans

- Finely chop white portion of onions and combine with cream cheese and blue cheese, blending well. Shape into a ball.
- Finely chop green portion of onions and combine with pecans and roll cheese ball in the mixture to completely cover.
- Chill at least 3 hours. Serve with crackers.

Olive Balls

2¼ cups shredded cheddar cheese

1⅓ cups flour

1 stick margarine, melted

34 small pimento stuffed olives, drained

- Mix cheese and flour; then add margarine.
- Form a small amount of dough mixture around each olive to cover. Shape into small balls. Place on ungreased cookie sheet and refrigerate for at least 1 hour.
- Bake at 400° for 15 minutes or until golden brown.

Ranch Cheese Ball

1 package dry ranch-style salad dressing mix

2 (8 ounce) packages cream cheese, softened

¼ cup finely chopped pecans

1 (3 ounce) jar real bacon bits

- With mixer, stir together the dressing mix and cream cheese.
- Roll into a ball. Roll cheese ball in the pecans and bacon bits.
- Refrigerate several hours before serving.

Spinach Cheese Ball

1 (10 ounce) package frozen chopped spinach, thawed

2 (8 ounce) packages cream cheese, softened

1 (1.2 ounce) package dry vegetable soup mix

1 (8 ounce) can water chestnuts, chopped

- Drain spinach on paper towels. Squeeze or mash spinach into towels several times to make sure all water is gone from the spinach.
- In mixer bowl, beat the cream cheese until smooth. Fold in the spinach, soup mix and water chestnuts.
- Form into a ball and serve with crackers.

Beefy Cheese Balls

2 (8 ounce) packages cream cheese, softened

2 (2½ ounce) jars dried beef

1 bunch fresh green onions with tops, chopped

1 teaspoon cayenne pepper

• Beat cream cheese with mixer until smooth and creamy.

• Chop dried beef in food processor or blender.

• Combine the beef, cream cheese, onions and cayenne pepper.

• Form into a ball and chill overnight.

Serve with crackers.

Jalapeno Bites

1 (12 ounce) can jalapeno peppers

2 cups grated cheddar cheese

4 eggs, beaten

¼ cup whole milk or cream

• Seed and chop peppers. Place peppers in greased 9-inch pie plate. Sprinkle cheese over peppers.

• Pour eggs over cheese. You may want to use salt and pepper on eggs.

• Bake at 375° for about 22 minutes. Cut into small slices to serve.

Bacon Roll-Ups

⅔ cup sour cream

½ teaspoon celery salt

½ pound bacon, cooked and crumbled

1 (8 ounce) package crescent rolls, separated

• Combine sour cream, celery salt and bacon. Spread over rolls and fold over. Bake at 375° for 10 to 15 minutes.

English Muffin Pizza

English muffin, split in half

Canned or bottled pizza sauce

Sliced salami or pepperoni

Grated mozzarella cheese or cheddar

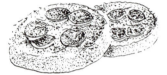

- Split muffin in half. Spread muffin with canned pizza sauce.
- Add salami or pepperoni.
- Top with grated cheese and place under broiler until cheese is melted and begins to bubble.

If you want to go all out, you can add any combination of the following ingredients: cooked chopped onion, cooked chopped green pepper, sliced jalapeno peppers and chopped green or black olives.

Sausage Rounds

1 (8 ounce) package crescent dinner rolls

1 pound sausage, uncooked

½ teaspoon garlic powder

½ cup grated cheddar cheese

- Open package of rolls and smooth out dough with a rolling pin, sealing the seams.
- Sprinkle dough with garlic powder and cheese.
- Break up sausage with hands and spread a thin layer of sausage over rolls. Roll into a log. Wrap in wax paper and freeze several hours.
- Slice into ¼-inch rounds.
- Place on cookie sheet and bake at 350° for 20 minutes or until lightly browned.

Stuffers

1 pound large mushrooms

1 cup cracker crumbs

3 tablespoons margarine, melted

2 slices ham lunch meat, finely chopped

- Remove stems and inside of mushrooms.
- Chop a few of the stems and mix with remaining ingredients.
- Stuff mushrooms and place in buttered casserole dish.
- Bake at 325° for 15 to 20 minutes.

Jack Quesadillas

¼ cup ricotta cheese

6 (6-inch) corn tortillas

⅔ cup shredded Monterey Jack cheese

1 (4 ounce) can diced green chilies, drained

- Spread about a tablespoon of ricotta over tortilla. Place a heaping tablespoon of cheese and add a tablespoon of chilies. Place a second tortilla over the top of that.
- Repeat to make 2 more quesadillas.
- In a heated skillet add 1 quesadilla and cook 3 minutes on each side. Remove from heat and cut into 4 wedges. Repeat with remaining quesadillas.

Serve warm with salsa.

Pigs in a Blanket

1 package of 10 wieners

3 cans biscuits (10 biscuits per can)

Dijon mustard

- Cut each wiener in thirds.
- Take each biscuit and flatten slightly and spread with mustard.
- Wrap each wiener piece in a biscuit; pinch to seal.
- Bake at 400° for 10 to 12 minutes.

Toasted Pepperoni

1 box melba toasts

¾ cup chili sauce

5 ounces pepperoni rounds

1 cup shredded mozzarella cheese

- Spread toast with chili sauce and top with pepperoni slices.
- Sprinkle with cheese and bake on cookie sheet at 375° for 3 to 5 minutes.

Water Chestnut Appetizers

1 (8 ounce) can water chestnuts

5 chicken livers, halved

5 thin slices bacon, halved

Sweet and hot mustard

- Divide water chestnuts into 10 portions.
- Wrap each chestnut and liver in a piece of bacon.
- Secure with toothpick and broil until bacon is crisp. Serve with sweet and hot mustard as a dip.

Party on the Rye

1 cup mayonnaise

¾ cup grated parmesan cheese

1 onion, finely grated

1 package party rye bread

- Combine mayonnaise, cheese and onion.
- Spread on bread and broil 2 to 3 minutes. Watch closely.

Cocktail Sausages

⅔ cup prepared mustard

1 cup plum jelly

½ teaspoon garlic powder

4 (4 ounce) cans Vienna
sausages, halved

- Mix mustard, jelly and garlic powder. Heat. Add sausages; heat thoroughly; serve hot.

Green Eyes

4 medium size dill
pickles

4 slices boiled ham

Light cream cheese,
softened

Black pepper

- Dry off pickles.
- Lightly coat one side of the ham slices with cream cheese and sprinkle on a little pepper.
- Roll the pickle up in the ham slice coated with cream cheese.
- Chill. Slice into circles to serve.

Cheddar Cheese Ring

2 (16 ounce) packages
shredded cheddar
cheese

1 small onion, finely
chopped

1 cup mayonnaise

1½ cups finely chopped
pecans

- Combine cheese, onion, mayonnaise and pecans. Press into an 8-inch ring mold. Cover with plastic wrap and refrigerate until set. Unmold when firm.
- Sprinkle top of cheese ring with additional chopped pecans.
- Slice to serve on wheat crackers.

Bacon Oyster Bites

1 (5 ounce) can smoked oysters, drained, chopped

⅔ cup herb-seasoned stuffing mix

¼ cup water

8 slices bacon, halved and partially cooked

- Combine oysters, stuffing mix and water. Add another teaspoon water if mixture seems too dry.

- Form into balls, using about 1 table-spoon mixture for each. Wrap a half slice of bacon around each and secure with a toothpick.

- Place on a rack in a shallow baking pan. Cook at 350° for 25 to 30 minutes.

Cheese in the Round

1 cup grated cheddar cheese

1 stick margarine, softened

1¼ cups flour

½ teaspoon cayenne pepper

- Combine all ingredients and form rolls 1-inch in diameter. Chill.

- When ready to bake, slice into ¼-inch rounds and bake at 375° for 5 to 8 minutes.

Garlic Shrimp

1 clove garlic, minced

⅔ cup chili sauce

½ pound thin bacon strips

1 pound medium shrimp, cooked

- Add garlic to chili sauce and set aside for several hours.

- Broil the bacon on one side only. Cut in half.

- Dip shrimp in the chili sauce and then wrap with half a bacon strip on the uncooked side out; fasten with tooth-picks. Refrigerate.

- Just before serving, broil shrimp until bacon is crisp.

Beefy Bites

1 (8 ounce) cream cheese, softened

1 teaspoon minced onion

1 (2 ½ ounce) dried beef, very finely chopped

¼ teaspoon garlic powder

- Mix cream cheese in mixer until creamy.
- Add remaining ingredients.
- Form into small bite-size balls and refrigerate. Serve with toothpicks.

Special Pimento Cheese

5 cups shredded sharp cheddar cheese

2 (4 ounce) jars diced pimentos, drained

1 cup salsa

3 tablespoons mayonnaise

- Combine grated cheese, pimentos and salsa in large bowl.
- Stir in mayonnaise, blending well. Store in refrigerator.

Homemade Pimento Cheese

2 cups cheddar cheese, grated

½ cup salad dressing (not mayonnaise)

2 tablespoons pimento, chopped

¼ teaspoon white vinegar

- Combine and mix together all the ingredients listed. Chill several hours, if possible, before serving.

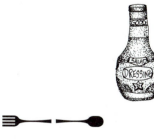

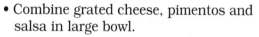

Holy Guacamole

4 avocados, peeled
½ cup salsa
¼ cup sour cream
1 teaspoon salt

- Split avocados and remove seeds. Mash avocado with a fork.
- Add salsa, sour cream and salt.

  Serve with tortilla chips.

Great Balls of Fire

1 pound lean hot sausage
3 green onions, chopped
1 can chopped tomatoes and green chilies
1 (2 pound) box Velveeta cheese

- Brown sausage in a large skillet. Drain off fat. Add onions, tomatoes and green chilies; mix.
- Cut cheese into chunks and add to sausage mixture; cook on low heat until cheese is melted. Serve hot in chafing dish with large chips.

Shrimp Squares

1 (6 ounce) can shrimp, drained, chopped
1 cup mayonnaise
1 cup shredded cheddar cheese
10-12 slices white bread, trimmed and cut in squares

- Combine the shrimp, mayonnaise and cheese.
- Spread shrimp mixture on the bread squares and broil until bubbly.

Mozzarella Picks

10 ounces mozzarella cheese, cut in strips

2 eggs, slightly beaten

2 tablespoons milk

2 cups fine cracker crumbs

• Dip the cheese cubes into the egg and milk. Roll in the cracker crumbs.

• Heat about 1 inch of oil in a skillet and fry the breaded cheese until browned. To serve, stick each cube with a toothpick.

Con Queso Chili

1 (2 pound) box Velveeta cheese, melted

2 (15 ounce) cans chili, no beans

1 (4 ounce) can green chilies

1 medium onion, finely chopped

• Mix all ingredients and pour into a 9-inch baking dish. Bake at 350° for 35 minutes.

Serve with chips.

Whiz Biz

1 (8 ounce) jar processed cheese spread

2 tablespoons dry white wine (or cooking wine)

1 teaspoon prepared mustard

1 teaspoon worcestershire sauce

• Mix all ingredients together. Chill. Serve with crackers.

Artichoke Bites

1½ cups mayonnaise

¾ cup freshly grated parmesan cheese

1 (4 ounce) can chopped green chilies

1 (14 ounce) jar artichoke hearts, chopped

- Mix mayonnaise, parmesan cheese, green chilies and artichoke hearts (remove any spikes or tough leaves from artichokes).
- Put 1 teaspoon of the mixture on bite-size toast rounds. Broil until lightly brown.

Bacon-Wrapped Water Chestnuts

1 (8 ounce) can whole water chestnuts, drained

¼ cup soy sauce

¼ teaspoon cayenne pepper

About ½ pound bacon, cut in thirds

- Marinate water chestnuts for an hour in soy sauce and cayenne.
- Wrap ⅓ slice bacon around the water chestnuts and fasten with a tooth pick.
- Bake at 375° for 20 minutes or until bacon is done. Drain and serve hot.

No-See-Um Chicken Livers

2 white onions, sliced

10-12 chicken livers

4 strips bacon

⅓ cup sherry

- Place onion slices in shallow pan. Top each onion slice with a chicken liver and ⅓ strip bacon. Pour sherry over all.
- Bake, uncovered at 350° for about 45 minutes or until bacon is crisp. Baste occasionally with pan drippings.

Border Queso

2 canned jalapeno peppers, reserve 1 tablespoon liquid

1 (2 pound) box Velveeta cheese

1 (4 ounce) jar pimentos, drained and chopped

3 fresh green onions, chopped

- Seed jalapeno peppers and chop very fine.
- Combine peppers, cheese, pimentos and onion in saucepan.
- Heat on stove, stirring constantly, until cheese melts. Stir in reserved liquid. Serve with tortilla chips.

Cheddar Puffs

1 stick margarine, softened

1 cup grated cheddar cheese

1¼ cups flour

¼ teaspoon salt

- Blend together the margarine and cheese until fairly smooth.
- Stir in flour and salt. Knead lightly with hands.
- Roll, a teaspoon at a time, into balls.
- Place on cookie sheet. Bake at 375° for 14 to 15 minutes or until golden. Serve hot.

Toasted Crab

¾ cup shredded cheddar cheese

1 stick margarine, softened

1 (6 ounce) can crabmeat, drained

6 English muffins, split in halves

- In a bowl, combine cheese, softened margarine and crabmeat; mix well.
- Spread mixture on each muffin half. Cut into quarters and place on cookie sheet.
- Broil for 5 minutes. Serve hot.

Bubbly Franks

1 package wieners

½ cup chili sauce

½ cup packed brown sugar

½ cup bourbon

- Cut wieners into bite-size pieces.
- Combine chili sauce, sugar and bourbon in a saucepan.
- Add wieners to sauce and simmer 30 minutes. Serve in chafing dish.

Cheese Straws

1 (5 ounce) package pie crust mix

¾ cup shredded cheddar cheese

Cayenne pepper

¼ teaspoon garlic powder

- Prepare pie crust according to package directions. Roll out into a rectangular shape.
- Sprinkle cheese over dough. Press the cheese into the dough. Sprinkle cayenne pepper and garlic over the cheese.
- Fold dough over once to cover cheese. Roll to make a ¼-inch thickness.
- Cut dough into ½ x 3-inch strips and place on a lightly greased cookie sheet.
- Bake at 350° for 12 to 15 minutes.

Cheddar Toppers

1 cup chopped black olives

1 cup shredded cheddar cheese

½ cup mayonnaise

½ cup finely minced green olives

- Combine all ingredients and mix well.
- To serve, spread mixture on English muffins. Bake at 350° for 30 minutes. After baking, quarter the muffins and serve as hors d'oeuvres.

Tortilla Rollers

1 (8 ounce) package cream cheese, softened

1 (4 ounce) can chopped black olives, drained

1 (4 ounce) can chopped green chilies, drained

1 (12 ounce) jar salsa

- With a mixer, beat cream cheese until smooth. Add black olives, green chilies and ¼ cup salsa, mixing well.

To serve, spread on flour tortillas and roll up. Refrigerate several hours. Slice in half-inch slices. Insert toothpick in each slice and dip in salsa.

Cheese It

1 (5 ounce) jar processed cheese spread, softened

½ stick butter, softened

½ cup flour

¼ teaspoon salt

- In mixer whip the cheese and butter, mixing flour and salt. Make a roll 1½ inches in diameter; place in freezer for 15 to 20 minutes.
- When chilled slice ½-inch thick to make small circles.
- Place on ungreased baking sheet and bake at 425° for 12 to 15 minutes.

Onion Crisps

2 sticks margarine, softened

2 cups shredded cheddar cheese

1 package dry onion soup mix

2 cups flour

- Combine all ingredients. Dough will be very thick.
- Divide into two batches and form into two rolls. Refrigerate for about 3 hours.
- Slice in ¼-thick slices.
- Bake at 350° for 12 to 15 minutes.

Sausage Bites

1 pound hot sausage

1 pound colby or cheddar cheese, grated

3¾ cups biscuit mix

½ teaspoon garlic powder

- Combine sausage, cheese, garlic powder and biscuit mix. Kneed thoroughly.
- Roll into 1-inch balls.
- Bake on a cookie sheet at 350° for 15 to 18 minutes until lightly browned.

Hot Cocktail Squares

1 (4 ounce) can chopped green chilies

1 (3 ounce) jar bacon bits

1 (16 ounce) package shredded cheddar cheese

7 eggs

- In a greased 7 x 11-inch baking dish, layer green chilies, bacon bits and cheese.
- Beat eggs with a fork until well beaten. Season with a little salt and several drops Tabasco. Pour over cheese.
- Bake covered at 350° for 25 minutes. Uncover and bake another 10 minutes. Serve warm.

Bits of Frank

1 package (8 count)
frankfurters

1 (8 ounce) package corn
muffin mix

½ teaspoon chili powder

⅔ cup milk

- Cut franks into 1-inch pieces.
- Combine corn muffin mix, chili powder and milk. Add the pieces of frankfurters to the corn muffin mix stirring well to coat each piece.
- Drop one at a time into deep hot fat. Fry for 2 minutes or until brown, drain. Serve warm with chili sauce for dunking.

Mexican Fudge

1 (16 ounce) package
shredded American
cheese

4 eggs, beaten

⅔ cup jalapeno green
sauce

1 teaspoon worcestershire

- In a sprayed 7x11-inch baking dish, spread ½ of the cheese in the dish.
- Combine eggs with green sauce and worcestershire and pour over cheese in the dish. Add the remaining cheese.
- Bake at 350° for 30 minutes.
- Cut into squares to serve. Can be served hot or room temperature.

Crispy Chestnuts

1 (8 ounce) can whole
water chestnuts

5-6 slices bacon,
quartered

Honey mustard

- Wrap each water chestnut with quartered strip of bacon. Secure with toothpick.
- Broil until bacon is cooked and removed.
- Dip in honey mustard.

Peanut Butter Sticks

1 loaf thin sliced
  sandwich bread

1 cup smooth peanut
  butter

½ cup peanut oil

1 teaspoon sugar, optional

- Trim crust from the bread. Cut each slice into four fingers. Place bread and the bread crust in separate pans.
- Bake at 200° for one hour or until crisp, turning often.
- In your food processor make crumbs from the dry bread crust.
- Mix peanut butter and oil. Dip bread fingers into peanut mixture, then roll in bread crumbs.
- Arrange in layers in an airtight container; let stand overnight. These must be stored in a tightly covered container.

Hot Artichoke Spread

1 (14 ounce) can
  artichoke hearts,
  drained, finely chopped

1 cup mayonnaise

1 cup grated parmesan
  cheese

1 package Italian salad
  dressing mix

- Chop artichoke and remove the tough outer leaves. Combine all ingredients, mixing thoroughly.
- Pour into a 9-inch square baking pan.
- Bake at 350° for 20 minutes.

Serve hot with assorted crackers.

Devil's Spread

1 (4¼ ounce) can deviled ham

¾ cup mayonnaise

1 tablespoon grated onion

1 (4 ounce) can chopped green chilies

• Mix all ingredients. Spread on wheat crackers.

Artichoke Spread

1 (14 ounce) jar marinated artichoke hearts

1 cup grated parmesan cheese

1 cup mayonnaise

1 teaspoon dried parsley

• Drain artichoke hearts and chop, removing the tough outer leaves. Combine artichokes, cheese, mayonnaise and parsley; blending well.

• Spoon into a non-stick sprayed 9-inch baking dish; bake at 350° for 20 minutes.

Serve with melba toast rounds.

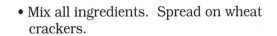

Smoky Gouda Spread

¾ cup chopped walnuts

1 (8 ounce) smoked gouda cheese

1 (8 ounce) package cream cheese, softened

¼ cup sliced green onions

• Spread walnuts in a shallow baking pan. Bake at 325° for 10 minutes or until lightly toasted. Cool and set aside.

• Trim and discard outer red edge of gouda cheese. Grate cheese. With mixer combine, the cream cheese and gouda cheese. Mixing well, stir in walnuts and onions.

Serve with apple wedges or crackers.

Jiffy Tuna Spread

1 (7 ounce) can white tuna, drained

½ cup chopped ripe olives

1 package dry Italian salad dressing mix

1 (8 ounce) carton sour cream

- Combine all ingredients, mixing well. Sprinkle with a little paprika for color and serve with crackers.

Cucumber Spread

1 cup seeded, chopped cucumbers

1 (8 ounce) package cream cheese, softened

½ cup mayonnaise

1 teaspoon seasoned salt

- Before chopping cucumber, make sure seeds have all been removed.
- With mixer, beat cream cheese until creamy; mix in mayonnaise, seasoned salt and cucumber.

Spread on crackers.

Crab Spread

Finely shredded lettuce

2 (8 ounce) packages cream cheese, room temperature

1 (12 ounce) bottle cocktail sauce

1 (6 ounce) can crab-meat, drained

- Arrange lettuce on small serving plate.
- Beat cream cheese with mixer; then fold in cocktail sauce and crabmeat.
- Spoon over lettuce. You may sprinkle a little garlic powder over crab, if you like.

Serve with toast points or crackers.

44

Black Olive Spread

1 (8 ounce) package cream cheese, softened

½ cup mayonnaise

1 (4 ounce) can chopped black olives, drained

3 green onions, chopped very fine

- Cream together the cream cheese and mayonnaise until smooth.
- Add olives and onions. Chill.

Spread on slices of party rye.

Pineapple Spread

2 (8 ounce) packages cream cheese

1 (8 ounce) can crushed pineapple, drained

¼ cup finely chopped sweet red pepper

1 teaspoon seasoned salt

- Combine cream cheese, pineapple, green pepper and sprinkle with salt.
- Roll into a ball and serve with crackers.
- Spread on Wheatsworth crackers.

Caramel Apple Dip

1 (8 ounce) package cream cheese, softened

1 cup packed brown sugar

1 teaspoon vanilla

½ cup chopped dry roasted peanuts

- Combine cream cheese, brown sugar and vanilla with mixer. Beat until creamy.
- Stir in peanuts.
- Refrigerate.

Serve with crisp apple slices.

Sweet Dip

1 (7 ounce) jar
marshmallow cream

1 (8 ounce) package
cream cheese

1 teaspoon ground
cinnamon

1 (14 ounce) can
sweetened condensed
milk

- In mixer bowl combine all ingredients and blend until smooth. Refrigerate for several hours.

Serve with fresh fruit.

Nutty Apple Dip

1 (8 ounce) package
cream cheese, softened

1 cup packed brown
sugar

1 teaspoon vanilla

1 cup finely chopped
pecans

- In a small mixing bowl combine cream cheese, sugar and vanilla. Beat until smooth.
- Stir in pecans.

Serve with sliced apples for dipping.

Orange Dip for Apples

1 (8 ounce) package
cream cheese, softened

1 (8 ounce) carton orange
yogurt

½ cup orange marmalade

¼ cup finely chopped
pecans

- In mixing bowl beat cream cheese until smooth.
- Fold in remaining ingredients. Refrigerate.

Serve with apple slices.

Orange Sour Cream Dip

1 (6 ounce) can frozen orange juice concentrate, thawed

1 (3.4 ounce) package vanilla instant pudding mix

1 cup milk

¼ cup sour cream

- Combine the orange juice concentrate, vanilla pudding mix and milk. Stir with a wire whisk until mixture is blended and smooth. Stir in sour cream.
- Cover and chill at least 2 hours.

  Serve with fresh fruit.

Chocolate Fruit Dip

1 (8 ounce) package cream cheese, softened

¼ cup chocolate syrup

1 (7 ounce) jar marshmallow cream

Fruit

- In a mixing bowl beat cream cheese and chocolate syrup until smooth.
- Fold in marshmallow cream.
- Cover and refrigerate until serving.

  Serve with apple wedges, banana chunks or strawberries.

Juicy Fruit Dip

1 (8 ounce) package cream cheese, softened

1 (7 ounce) jar marshmallow cream

¼ teaspoon ground ginger

- Cream together with the mixer, the cream cheese and marshmallow cream; fold in ginger.
- Chill.

  Serve with apple slices, pineapple sticks, honeydew slices, etc.

Peanut Butter Spread

1 (8 ounce) package
  cream cheese, softened

1 ⅔ cups creamy peanut
  butter

½ cup powdered sugar

1 tablespoon milk

• In mixer, cream together all ingredients.
  Serve spread with apple wedges or
  graham crackers.

Fruit Dip for Nectarines

1 (8 ounce) package
  cream cheese, softened

2 (7 ounce) cartons
  marshmallow cream

¼ teaspoon cinnamon

⅛ teaspoon ground ginger

• With mixer, combine and beat together
  all ingredients. Mix well. Refrigerate.
  Serve with unpeeled slices of
  nectarines or any other fruit.

Fruit Dip

1 (8 ounce) carton sour
  cream

3 heaping tablespoons
  brown sugar

½ teaspoon ground
  cinnamon

Dash ground ginger

• Mix sour cream, brown sugar and
  cinnamon.

• Serve with fresh fruit.

Amaretto Dip

1 (8 ounce) package
cream cheese, softened

¼ cup amaretto liqueur

¼ cup chopped slivered
almonds, toasted

Banana bread

• With mixer blend cream cheese and
amaretto. Stir in the toasted almonds.
Serve with crackers or sliced apples.

*This is also a good spread on
banana bread, zucchini bread, etc.*

Deviled Pecans

½ stick butter, melted (no
margarine)

1 tablespoon
worcestershire

2 cups pecan halves

¼ teaspoon cayenne
pepper

• In a mixing bowl combine the butter and
the worcestershire and mix well.

• Add pecans, pepper and ¼ teaspoon
salt. Stir and toss pecans until well
coated.

• Roast on cookie sheet at 350° for 15
minutes, stirring or shaking the pan
occasionally.

Classy Red Pecans

½ stick margarine or
butter

1½ teaspoons chili
powder

¾ teaspoon garlic salt

3 cups pecan halves

• In large skillet, melt butter. Stir in chili
powder, garlic salt and pecans.

• Cook on medium heat, stirring pecans
constantly for 4 or 5 minutes until
browned and well coated with chili
powder.

Cinnamon Pecans

1 pound pecan halves

1 egg white, slightly
beaten with fork

2 tablespoons cinnamon

¾ cup sugar

- Combine the pecan halves with the egg white and mix well.

- Sprinkle with mixture of the cinnamon and sugar. Stir until all pecans are coated.

- Spread on a cookie sheet and bake at 325° for about 20 minutes. Cool. Store in a covered container.

Toasted Pecans

12 cups pecan halves

1 stick margarine

Salt

½ teaspoon garlic powder

- Place pecans in a large baking pan. In 250° oven, toast pecans for 30 minutes to dry.

- Slice margarine and melt in baking pan. Let pecans get completely greasy, stirring twice.

- After pecans and margarine have mixed well, sprinkle with salt and garlic powder and stir often.

- Toast pecans one hour until margarine has been absorbed and pecans are crisp.

Sugar Coated Peanuts

1½ cups sugar

1 tablespoon maple
  flavoring

4½ cups Spanish peanuts

1½ teaspoon salt

- In a large saucepan combine the sugar, ¾ cup water, maple flavoring and peanuts. Stir over medium heat for 20 minutes or until almost all of the liquid is absorbed.

- Spread on a greased 10 x 15-inch baking pan and sprinkle with salt. Bake at 350° for about 25 minutes or until peanuts are well coated, stirring 2 to 3 times.

- Remove to a wax paper-lined baking sheet to cool. Store in airtight container.

Best Punch

1 (46 ounce) can
pineapple juice

1 (46 ounce) can apricot
nectar

3 (6 ounce) cans frozen
limeade concentrate,
thawed

3 quarts ginger ale,
chilled

• Combine the first three juices and
refrigerate. When ready to serve, add
ginger ale.

Easiest Grape Punch

½ gallon ginger ale

Red seedless grapes

Sparkling white grape
juice, chilled

• Make an ice ring of the ginger ale and
seedless grapes.

• When ready to serve, pour sparkling
white grape juice in punch bowl with ice
ring.

*Sparkling white grape juice is great
just by itself!*

Great Punch

1 (46 ounce) can
pineapple juice

2 (46 ounce) cans apple
juice

3 quarts ginger ale

Fresh mint to garnish,
optional

• Combine pineapple juice and apple juice
and make an ice ring with part of the
juice.

• Chill remaining juice and ginger ale.

• When ready to serve, combine juices
and ginger ale and place ice ring in
punch bowl.

Perfect Party Punch

1 (12 ounce) can frozen
  limeade concentrate

1 (46 ounce) can
  pineapple juice, chilled

1 (46 ounce) apricot
  nectar, chilled

1 quart ginger ale, chilled

• Dilute the limeade concentrate as
  directed on the can.

• Add the pineapple juice and apricot
  nectar, stirring well.

• When ready to serve,
  add the ginger ale.

Ruby Red Punch

1 (46 ounce) can
  pineapple-grapefruit
  juice

½ cup sugar

¼ cup cinnamon candies

1 quart ginger ale, chilled

• In a large saucepan, combine pineapple-
  grapefruit juice, sugar and candies.
  Bring to a boil, stirring until candies are
  dissolved.

• Cool until time to serve, stirring occasionally, to completely dissolve candies.

• Add ginger ale just before serving.

Cranberry Punch

2 (28 ounce) bottles
  ginger ale, chilled

1 (48 ounce) can
  pineapple juice, chilled

1 quart cranberry juice,
  chilled

1 quart pineapple
  sherbet, broken up

• Pour all ingredients in punch bowl.
  Serve.

Creamy Strawberry Punch

1 (10 ounce) package
frozen strawberries,
thawed

½ gallon strawberry ice
cream, softened

2 (2 liter) bottles ginger
ale, chilled

Fresh strawberries to
garnish, optional

- Process strawberries through blender.
- Combine strawberries, chunks of ice cream and the ginger ale in punch bowl.
- Stir and serve immediately.

Mocha Punch

4 cups brewed coffee

¼ cup sugar

4 cups milk

4 cups chocolate ice
cream, softened

- In a container, combine coffee and sugar; stir until sugar is dissolved. Refrigerate for 2 hours.
- Just before serving, pour into a small punch bowl.
- Add milk; mix well. Top with scoops of ice cream and stir well.

Pink Punch

3 (6 ounce) cans frozen
pink lemonade
concentrate, undiluted

1 (750 milliliter) bottle
pink sparkling wine

3 (2 liter) bottles lemon-
lime carbonated
beverage, divided

Lime slices to garnish,
optional

- Stir together all ingredients, except 1 bottle carbonated beverage, in an airtight container; cover and freeze 8 hours or until firm.
- Let stand at room temperature 10 minutes; place in a punch bowl.
- Add remaining bottle carbonated beverage, stirring until slushy.

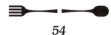

Strawberry Punch

2 (10 ounce) boxes frozen strawberries, thawed

2 (6 ounce) cans frozen pink lemonade concentrate

2 (2 liter) bottles ginger ale, chilled

Fresh strawberries to garnish, optional

- Process strawberries through blender.
- Pour lemonade into punch bowl and stir in strawberries.
- Add chilled ginger ale and stir well.

  It would be nice to make an ice ring out of another bottle of ginger ale.

Party Punch

1 (46 ounce) can pineapple juice

1 (46 ounce) can apple juice

3 quarts ginger ale, chilled

Pineapple chunks to garnish, optional

- Combine pineapple and apple juice in a very large plastic container or any container large enough to hold both juices. You can use two plastic pitchers. Freeze both juices.
- When ready to serve, place pineapple and apple juice in punch bowl and add the chilled ginger ale. Stir to mix.

Cranberry Lemon Punch

2 quarts cranberry juice

1 (6 ounce) can lemonade concentrate, thawed

⅔ cup maraschino cherry juice

2 liters lemon lime soda, chilled

- Combine all ingredients.

  It would be good to have ice ring made out of cranberry juice, lemon slices and maraschino cherries.

Pina Colada Punch

1 (46 ounce) can pineapple juice, chilled

1 (20 ounce) can crushed pineapple, undrained

1 (15 ounce) can cream of coconut

1 (32 ounce) bottle 7-Up, chilled

• Combine all ingredients.
• Serve over ice cubes.

Wine Punch

2 quarts ginger ale, chilled

2 (12 ounce) cans frozen limeade concentrate

4 limeade cans white wine, chilled

Lime slices

• Make an ice ring with as much ginger ale as necessary.
• Combine limeade, white wine and remaining ginger ale in punch bowl.
• Serve with ice ring and lime slices.

Sparkling Punch

6 oranges, unpeeled, thinly sliced

1 cup sugar

2 (750 milliliter) bottles dry white wine

3 (750 milliliter) bottles sparkling wine, chilled

• Place orange slices in a large plastic or glass container and sprinkle with sugar.
• Add white wine; cover and chill at least 8 hours.
• Stir in sparkling wine.

Champagne Punch

1 (750 ml) bottle
champagne, chilled

1 (32 ounce) bottle ginger
ale, chilled

1 (6 ounce) can frozen
orange juice
concentrate

Orange slices to garnish,
optional

• Mix all ingredients in punch bowl.
Serve chilled.

Apple Party Punch

3 cups sparkling apple
cider

2 cups apple juice

1 cup pineapple juice

½ cup brandy

• Combine all ingredients and freeze 8
hours.

• Remove punch from freezer 30 minutes
before serving.

• Place in a small punch bowl and break
into chunks. Stir until slushy.

Egg Nog

1 gallon egg nog

1 pint whipping cream

1 quart brandy

½ gallon ice cream,
softened

• Mix all ingredients.

• Serve in individual cups and sprinkle
with nutmeg and serve immediately.

Amaretto Cooler

1¼ cups amaretto

2 quarts cold orange juice

1 (15 ounce) bottle club soda, chilled

Orange slices to garnish, optional

• Combine all ingredients, stirring well. Serve over ice.

Creamy Orange Drink

1¾ cups milk

½ pint vanilla ice cream

⅓ cup frozen orange juice concentrate

1 teaspoon non-dairy creamer

• In blender, combine all ingredients.

• Blend until smooth.

Banana Split Float

2 ripe bananas, mashed

3 cups milk

1 (10 ounce) package frozen sweetened strawberries, thawed

1½ pints chocolate ice cream, divided

• Place bananas in blender and add milk, strawberries and ½ pint of the chocolate ice cream. Beat just until blended.

• Pour into tall, chilled glasses and top each with a scoop of chocolate ice cream.

Lemonade Milk Shake

1 (6 ounce) can frozen lemonade concentrate, thawed

1 cup diced bananas

1 quart vanilla ice cream

3 cups milk

- In mixing bowl, combine lemonade concentrate and bananas. Beat until it is a heavy consistency.
- For each milk shake, add one scoop vanilla ice cream and ¼ cup of lemon-banana mixture in bottom of glass.
- Fill glass ⅔ full of milk and stir until blended. Top it off with one more scoop of ice cream.

Peanut Power Shake

2 bananas, cut up

½ cup frozen orange juice concentrate, thawed

¼ cup peanut butter

¼ cup milk

- In blender container, combine all ingredients. Cover and blend until smooth.
- Add 1 cup of ice cubes, blending until smooth.

Purple Shakes

1 (6 ounce) can frozen grape juice concentrate

1 cup milk

2½ cups vanilla ice cream

2 tablespoons sugar, optional

- In blender combine all ingredients. Cover and blend at high speed for 30 seconds. Serve immediately.

Kahlua Frosty

1 cup kahlua

1 pint vanilla ice cream

1 cup half-and-half

¼ teaspoon almond extract

- In a blender, combine all ingredients and one heaping cup of ice cubes.
- Blend until smooth. Serve immediately.

Orange Lush

2 (6 ounce) cans frozen orange juice concentrate, thawed

1 pint cranberry juice

½ cup sugar

1 quart club soda

- Combine orange juice, cranberry juice and sugar, mixing thoroughly.
- Just before serving, pour into punch bowl and stir in the chilled club soda.

Fruit Smoothie

1 cup orange juice

1 ripe banana, peeled, thickly sliced

1 ripe peach, cut into chunks

1 cup strawberries

- Put the orange juice into a blender.
- Add the banana, peach, strawberries and 1 cup of ice cubes.
- Blend on high speed until liquefied.

Fruit Shake

2 (8 ounce) cartons
vanilla yogurt

1 cup fresh frozen
blueberries

1 cup fresh frozen peach
slices

1 (8 ounce) can pineapple
chunks, drained

- Process all ingredients in a blender until smooth, stopping to scrape down sides.
- Serve immediately.

Limeade Cooler

1½ pints lime sherbet

1 (6 ounce) can frozen
limeade concentrate

3 cups milk

Lime slices to garnish,
optional

- Beat lime sherbet in mixing bowl; add concentrated limeade and milk.
- Blend all ingredients together.
- Pour into 5 glasses, topping each with an additional scoop of lime sherbet. Serve immediately.

Pineapple Strawberry Cooler

2 cups milk

1 (20 ounce) can crushed
pineapple, chilled

½ pint vanilla ice cream

1 pint strawberry ice
cream

- In a mixer bowl, combine milk, pineapple and vanilla ice cream.
- Mix just until blended. Pour into tall glasses and top with a scoop of strawberry ice cream.

Strawberry Smoothie

2 bananas, peeled, sliced

1 pint fresh strawberries, quartered

1 (8 ounce) container strawberry yogurt

¼ cup orange juice

• Place all ingredients in blender. Process until smooth.

Orange Slush

2 cups orange juice

½ cup instant, non-fat dry milk

¼ teaspoon almond extract

8 ice cubes

• Add all ingredients in blender and process on high until mixture is combined and thickened. Serve immediately.

Victorian Iced Tea

4 individual tea bags

¼ cup sugar

1 (11 ounce) can frozen cranberry-raspberry juice concentrate, thawed

4 cups cold water

• Place tea bags in a teapot; add 4 cups boiling water. Cover and steep for 5 minutes.

• Remove and discard tea bags. Add sugar mix. Refrigerate tea.

• Just before serving, combine cranberry-raspberry concentrate and cold water in a 2½-quart pitcher; stir in tea. Serve with ice cubes.

Lemonade Tea

2 family-size tea bags
½ cup sugar
1 (12 ounce) can frozen lemonade
1 quart ginger ale, chilled

- Steep tea in 3 quarts water; then mix with sugar and lemonade.
- Add ginger ale just before serving.

Spiced Iced Tea

2 quarts tea
⅔ cup sugar
1 (12 ounce) can frozen lemonade concentrate, thawed
1 quart ginger ale

- Combine tea, sugar and lemonade; chill.
- Just before serving, add the chilled ginger ale.

Frosted Chocolate Milk

2 pints coffee ice cream
½ cup chocolate syrup
¼ cup instant coffee flakes
2 quarts milk, divided

- In a blender, beat ice cream, chocolate syrup, coffee and about half of the milk. Beat until well blended.
- Combine the remaining milk and chill before serving.
- Serve in frosted glasses.

Coffee Milk Shake

1 pint vanilla ice cream, divided

¼ cup milk

½ cup chocolate coated toffee bits

- In blender combine half the ice cream and all the milk. Cover and blend until combined.
- Add remaining ice cream. Cover and blend until desired consistency.
- Add toffee bits and process briefly with on/off pulse to mix.

Chocolate Yogurt Malt

4 cups frozen vanilla yogurt

1 cup chocolate milk

¼ cup instant chocolate malted milk drink

Mini-chocolate chips, optional

- Process all ingredients in a blender until smooth, stopping to scrape down sides.
- Serve immediately.
- Top with mini-chocolate chips.

Spanish Coffee

1 tablespoon sugar

4 cups hot, brewed coffee

¾ cup kahlua,

Sweetened whipped cream

- Stir sugar into hot coffee and add kahula.
- Pour into 4 serving cups.
- Top with whipped cream.

I

Instant Cocoa Mix

1 (8 quart) box dry milk powder

1 (12 ounce) jar non-dairy creamer

1 (16 ounce) can instant chocolate flavored drink mix

1¼ cups powdered sugar

- Combine all ingredients and store in an airtight container.
- To serve, use ¼ cup cocoa mix per cup of hot water.

Amaretto

3 cups sugar

1 pint vodka

3 tablespoons almond extract

1 tablespoon vanilla (not the imitation)

- Combine sugar and 2¼ cups water in a large pan. Bring mixture to a boil.
- Reduce heat. Let simmer 5 minutes, stirring occasionally. Remove from stove.
- Add vodka, almond and vanilla extracts. Stir to mix.
- Store in airtight jar.

Hot Cranberry Cider

1½ quarts cranberry juice

1 (12 ounce) can frozen orange juice concentrate, thawed

1½ orange juice cans water

½ teaspoon cinnamon

- Combine cranberry juice, orange juice and water in large saucepan. Bring to a boil to blend flavors.
- Add cinnamon, stirring well. Serve hot.

Peppermint Hot Chocolate

3 cups hot milk, divided

8 small chocolate peppermint patties

Pinch salt

1 cup half-and-half

- Combine ½ cup hot milk with chocolate peppermint patties, stirring well.
- Add pinch of salt and remaining hot milk.
- Heat to simmering, but do not boil.
- Add the cream.

Spiced Coffee

1 cup instant coffee

4 teaspoons grated lemon peel

4 teaspoons ground cinnamon

1 teaspoon ground cloves

- In a small jar, combine all ingredients; cover tightly.
- For each serving, spoon 2 teaspoons of coffee mix into coffee cup and stir in ¾ cup boiling water. Sweeten to taste.

Mexican Coffee

1 ounce kahlua

1 cup hot black coffee

Ground cinnamon

Sweetened whipped cream

- Pour kahlua and coffee into a tall mug.
- Sprinkle with cinnamon and stir.
- Top with whipped cream. (You can substitute frozen whipped topping).

Kid's Cherry Sparkler

2 (6 ounce) jars red
  maraschino cherries,
  drained

2 (6 ounce) jars green
  maraschino cherries,
  drained

½ gallon distilled water

1 (2 liter) bottle cherry
  7-Up, chilled

• Place 1 red or green cherry in each
  compartment of 4 ice cube trays.

• Fill trays with distilled water; freeze for
  8 hours. Serve soft drink over ice
  cubes.

Notes:

BREADS, BREAKFAST & BRUNCH

Cream Biscuits

2 cups flour

3 teaspoons baking powder

½ teaspoon salt

1 (8 ounce) carton whipping cream

- Combine flour, baking powder and salt.
- In mixer bowl, beat the whipping cream only until it holds a shape.
- Combine the flour mixture and cream; mix with a fork. Put dough on a lightly floured board and knead it for about 1 minute.
- Pat dough to a ¾-inch thickness. Cut out biscuits with a small biscuit cutter.
- Place on baking sheet; bake at 375° for about 12 minutes or until lightly brown.

Whipping Cream Biscuits

2½ cups biscuit mix

½ pint whipping cream

- Mix biscuit mix and cream. Place on a floured board. Knead several times.
- Pat out to ½-inch thickness. Cut with a biscuit cutter.
- Bake at 375° for 12 to 15 minutes or until lightly brown.

Drunk Biscuits

3¼ cups biscuit mix

¼ teaspoon salt

1 teaspoon sugar

1⅔ cups beer

- Combine all ingredients and spoon into 12 greased muffin cups.
- Bake at 400° for 15 to 20 minutes until golden.

Sour Cream Biscuits

⅓ cup club soda
⅓ cup sour cream
½ tablespoon sugar
2 cups of biscuit mix

- In a mixing bowl combine all ingredients stirring with a fork just until the dry ingredients are moistened.
- Turn bowl out onto lightly floured board and knead lightly several times.
- Roll dough into a 1-inch thickness and cut with a biscuit cutter.
- Place dough in a greased 9 x 13-inch baking pan. Bake at 400° for 12 to 14 minutes or until golden brown.

Refrigerator Biscuits

1 (8 ounce) package cream cheese, softened
1 stick margarine, softened
1 cup self-rising flour

- Beat cream cheese and margarine at medium speed with mixer for 2 minutes. Gradually add flour, beating at low speed, just until blended.
- Spoon dough into miniature muffin pans, filling ⅔ full or you can refrigerate dough for up to 3 days.
- Bake at 375° for 15 minutes or until golden brown.

Garlic Biscuits

5 cups biscuit mix

1 cup shredded cheddar cheese

1 (14 ounce) can chicken broth with roasted garlic

- Mix all ingredients to form a soft dough. Drop by heaping spoonfuls onto greased baking sheet.

- Bake at 425° for 10 minutes or until slightly brown.

Maple Biscuits

2¼ cups baking mix

⅔ cup milk

1½ cups maple syrup

- Combine baking mix and milk. Stir just until moistened. On a floured surface roll dough into ½-inch thickness. Cut with a 2-inch biscuit cutter.

- Pour syrup into a 7 x 11-inch baking dish. Place biscuits on top of syrup.

- Bake at 425° for 13 to 15 minutes or until biscuits are golden brown.

Serve with breakfast.

Speedy Biscuits

6 tablespoons shortening

3 cups self-rising flour

1 cup milk

Butter

- Cut shortening into the flour with a pastry cutter or by hand. Add milk and mix until dough forms a ball. Knead until dough is smooth.

- Place on a floured surface and flatten slightly. Cut with a floured biscuit cutter and place in a well greased pan, turning to grease both sides of the biscuits.

- Bake in a 400° oven for 10 to 12 minutes.

Hot Biscuits

1⅓ cup self-rising flour

1 (8 ounce) carton
whipping cream

2 tablespoons sugar

Butter

- Combine all ingredients and stir until blended.
- Drop biscuits by teaspoon onto a greased baking sheet.
- Bake at 400° for about 10 minutes or until lightly brown.
- Serve with plain or flavored butters on pages 84 and 85.

Fast Biscuits

2 cups self-rising flour

4 tablespoons
mayonnaise

1 cup milk

Butter

- Mix all ingredients and drop by spoon on a cookie sheet.
- Bake at 425° until biscuits are golden brown.
- Serve with plain or flavored butters on pages 84 and 85.

Date Biscuits

1 cup chopped dates

2 cups biscuit mix

½ cup grated American
cheese

¾ cup milk

- Combine dates, biscuit mix and cheese.
- Add milk; stir well to a moderately soft dough. Drop by teaspoonful onto a greased baking sheet.
- Bake in a 400° oven for 12 to 15 minutes. Serve hot.

Cream Cheese Biscuits

1 (3 ounce) package
  cream cheese, softened
1 stick butter, softened
1 cup self-rising flour
¼ teaspoon salt, optional

- In mixer beat cream cheese and butter together. Add flour, mixing well.
- Roll out to ½-inch thickness and cut with a small biscuit cutter.
- Place on a greased baking sheet and bake at 350° for 20 minutes or until lightly browned.

Hot Cheese Biscuits

1 small jar Old English
  cheese spread
½ stick margarine,
  softened
½ cup flour
⅛ teaspoon salt

- Mash cheese spread and the margarine, mixing well. Add flour and salt.
- Mix well. Roll into small balls. Chill one hour.
- Place on ungreased cookie sheet.
- Bake at 400° for 10 minutes. Balls will flatten as they cook. Serve hot.

Sausage Biscuits

1 (8 ounce) package
  grated cheddar cheese
1 pound hot bulk pork
  sausage
2 cups biscuit mix
¾ cup milk

- Combine first three ingredients. Add milk and stir well.
- Drop on ungreased cookie sheet.
- Bake at 400° until lightly brown. Serve hot.

Strawberry Topping for Biscuits

3½ cups sugar

1 (10 ounce) carton frozen strawberries, thawed

1 (6 ounce) can frozen orange juice concentrate, thawed

2 tablespoons lemon juice

• Combine sugar and strawberries in a large saucepan, mixing well. Over high heat bring to a full rolling boil. Boil one minute, stirring constantly.

• Remove from heat and stir in orange juice concentrate and lemon juice. Return to heat and bring to a boil for one minute, stirring constantly.

• Skim off foam off top. You could add red food coloring if you like.

• Pour into jelly glasses and seal with hot paraffin.

This is delicious over hot biscuits.

Onion Biscuits

2 cups biscuit mix

¼ cup milk

1 (8 ounce) container french onion dip

2 tablespoons finely minced green onion

• Mix all ingredients together until soft dough forms. Drop dough onto a greased cookie sheet.

• Bake at 400° for about 10 minutes or until light golden brown.

Toasted French Bread

1 unsliced loaf French bread

1 stick butter, softened

¾ cup parmesan cheese

1½ teaspoons Tabasco

- Slice bread in half lengthwise, then quarter.
- Combine butter, parmesan cheese and Tabasco. Spread on top of slices using all the mixture. Place on cookie sheet.
- Cook at 325° for about 25 minutes or until heated thoroughly and browned on top.

Parmesan Bread Deluxe

1 loaf unsliced Italian bread

½ cup refrigerated creamy Caesar dressing and dip

⅓ cup grated parmesan cheese

3 tablespoons finely chopped green onions

- Cut 24 (½-inch thick) slices from bread. Reserve remaining bread for other use.
- In small bowl, combine dressing, cheese and onion. Spread a teaspoon of dressing mixture onto each bread slice.
- Place bread on baking sheet. Broil 4-inches from heat until golden brown. Serve warm.

Bacon Cheese French Bread

1 (16 ounce) loaf unsliced french bread

5 slices bacon, cooked, crumbled

8 ounces mozzarella cheese, shredded

1 stick margarine, melted

- Slice loaf of bread into 1-inch slices. Place sliced loaf on a large piece of aluminum foil.
- Combine bacon and cheese. Sprinkle bacon and cheese in between slices of bread.
- Drizzle margarine over loaf, letting some drip down in between slices. Wrap loaf tightly in foil. Bake at 350° for 20 minutes or until thoroughly heated. Serve hot.

Ranch French Bread

1 loaf unsliced French bread

1 stick margarine, softened

1 tablespoon ranch-style dressing mix

1 tablespoon mayonnaise, optional

- Cut loaf in half horizontally. Blend margarine and dressing mix.
- Spread margarine mixture on bread.
- Wrap bread in foil. Bake at 350° for 15 minutes.

Cheese Bread

2 cups shredded sharp cheddar cheese

1 cup mayonnaise

1 envelope ranch-style mix

10 (1-inch) slices French bread

- Combine cheese, mayonnaise and dressing mix.
- Spread on bread slices and heat in oven until brown.

Chili Bread

1 loaf Italian bread,
   unsliced
1 stick margarine, melted
1 (4 ounce) can diced
   green chilies, drained
¾ cup grated Monterey
   Jack cheese

- Slice bread almost all the way through.
- Combine melted margarine, chilis and cheese. Spread between bread slices.
- Cover loaf with foil. Bake at 350° for 25 minutes.

Crunchy Bread Sticks

1 package hot dog buns
2 sticks margarine,
   melted
Garlic powder
Paprika

- Take each half bun and slice in half lengthwise.
- Using a pastry brush, butter all breadsticks and sprinkle a light amount of garlic powder and a couple of sprinkles of paprika.
- Place on cookie sheet and bake at 225° for about 45 minutes.

Butter Bread

2 sticks salted butter,
   softened
2 cups self-rising flour
1 (8 ounce) carton sour
   cream

- Combine all ingredients, mixing well.
- Drop by teaspoons into miniature muffin cups.
- Bake at 350° for 20 minutes or until lightly browned.

Beer Bread

3 cups self-rising flour

¼ cup sugar

12 ounces beer, at room temperature

1 stick margarine, melted

- Combine the flour, sugar and beer, mixing thoroughly.
- Pour into a greased 9 x 5-inch loaf pan. Bake at 350° for 35 minutes.
- Punch holes in top of bread. Pour melted margarine over top and bake another 10 minutes.

Cheese Sticks

1 loaf thick sliced bread

1 stick margarine, melted

1 cup grated cheddar cheese

1½ teaspoons paprika

- Remove crust from bread and slice into sticks.
- Brush or roll in melted margarine. Place on cookie sheet.
- Sprinkle on cheddar and paprika.
- Bake 325° for 20 minutes.

Butter Rolls

2 cups biscuit mix

1 (8 ounce) carton sour cream

1 stick butter, melted

- Combine all ingredients and mix well. Spoon into greased muffin tins and fill only half full.
- Bake at 400° for 12 to 14 minutes or lightly brown.

Onion Loaf

2 tablespoons instant minced onions

1 tablespoon poppy seed

1 stick margarine, melted

2 cans refrigerated butter flake biscuits

- Combine the onions and poppy seed with the margarine.
- Separate each biscuit into 2 or 3 rolls. Dip each piece in the margarine mixture, turning to coat.
- Place rolls on edge of a loaf pan arranging rolls into two rows. Pour any remaining margarine mixture over top of loaf.
- Bake at 325° for 35 minutes. Serve warm.

Tea Cakes

1 cup self-rising flour

1 cup whipping cream (not whipped)

2 tablespoons sugar

⅛ teaspoon ground cinnamon

- Combine all ingredients and pour into greased mini muffin cups.
- Bake at 375° for 10 to 15 minutes.

Cheese Drops

2 cups baking mix

⅔ cup milk

⅔ cup grated sharp cheddar cheese

½ stick margarine, melted

- Spray cookie sheet with non-stick spray.
- Mix together the baking mix, milk and cheese. Drop one heaping tablespoon of dough for each biscuit onto cookie sheet.
- Bake at 400° for 10 minutes or until slightly browned.
- While warm, brush tops of biscuits with the melted margarine. Serve hot.

Bread Sticks

1½ cups shredded monterey jack cheese

¼ cup poppy seeds

2 tablespoons dry onion soup mix

2 (11 ounce) cans bread-stick dough

- Spread cheese evenly in a 9 x 13-inch baking dish. Sprinkle poppy seeds and soup mix evenly over cheese.
- Separate breadstick dough into sticks. Stretch strips slightly until each strip is about 12 inches long.
- Place strips one at a time into the cheese mixture. Turn to coat all sides.
- Cut into 3 or 4-inch strips. Place on a cookie sheet and bake at 375° for about 12 minutes.

Spicy Cornbread Twists

⅓ stick margarine

⅓ cup cornmeal

¼ teaspoon red pepper

1 (11 ounce) can refrigerated soft breadsticks

- Place margarine in a pie plate and melt in oven. Remove from oven.
- On a piece of waxed paper, mix corn-meal and red pepper.
- Roll breadsticks in margarine and then in cornmeal mixture.
- Twist the breadsticks as label directs and place on a cookie sheet. Bake at 350° 15 to 18 minutes.

Corn Sticks

2 cups biscuit mix

1 (8 ounce) can cream-style corn

Melted butter

2 tablespoons minced green onion

- Mix biscuit mix, green onions and cream-style corn.
- Place dough on a floured surface and cut into 3 x 1-inch strips. Roll in melted butter.
- Bake at 400° 15 to 16 minutes.

Sausage Cornbread

1 (10½ ounce) can condensed golden corn soup

2 eggs

1 (8 ounce) package corn muffin mix

⅓ pound pork sausage, crumbled, cooked

- In a medium bowl combine soup, eggs and ¼ cup water or milk.
- Stir in corn muffin mix just until blended. Fold in sausage.
- Pour mixture into a greased 9-inch baking pan.
- Bake at 375° for 25 minutes or until golden brown. Cut into squares.

Mexican Cornbread

½ pound Mexican Velveeta cheese

¼ cup milk

2 (8 ounce) packages corn muffin mix

2 eggs, beaten

- In a saucepan, melt cheese with milk over low heat.
- In a bowl, combine corn muffin mix and eggs. Fold in cheese, mixing just until moistened.
- Pour into a greased 9 x 13-inch baking pan. Bake at 375° for about 25 minutes or until lightly brown.

Mayo Muffins

1¼ cup self-rising flour

3 tablespoons mayonnaise

1 cup whole milk

- Mix all ingredients together and spoon into greased muffin tins.
- Bake at 375° for 20 minutes or until lightly browned.

Filled Muffins

1 box blueberry muffin
   mix
1 egg
⅓ cup red raspberry jam
¼ cup sliced almonds

- Rinse blueberries and drain.
- In bowl, combine the muffin mix, egg and ½ cup water. Stir until moistened; break up any lumps in the mix.
- Place paper liners in 8 muffin cups. Fill cups half full of the batter.
- Combine the raspberry jam with the blueberries. Spoon mixture on top of batter. Cover with remaining batter. Sprinkle almonds over batter.
- Bake at 375 ° for about 18 minutes or until lightly brown.

Ginger Raisin Muffins

1 box gingerbread mix
1¼ cups lukewarm water
1 egg
2 (1½ ounce) boxes
   seedless raisins

• Combine gingerbread mix, water and egg, mixing well. Stir in raisins.
• Pour into greased muffin tins filled half full.
• Bake at 350° for 20 minutes or when tested done with a toothpick.

Blueberry Orange Muffins

1 package blueberry
   muffin mix
2 egg whites
½ cup orange juice
Orange marmalade

• Wash blueberries with cold water and drain.
• Mix together the muffin mix, egg whites and orange juice; break up any lumps. Fold blueberries gently into batter.
• Pour into muffin tins (with paper liners) about ½ full.
• Bake at 375° for 18 to 20 minutes until toothpick inserted in center comes out clean.
• Top with orange marmalade spooned over top of hot muffins.

Honey Cinnamon Butter

2 sticks butter
½ cup honey
1 teaspoon ground
   cinnamon
Breakfast breads

• Combine all ingredients in a small mixing bowl; beat until smooth.

Serve with muffins, toast, French toast or pancakes. Refrigerate any leftovers.

Orange Butter

⅔ cup butter (not margarine), room temperature

¼ cup frozen orange juice concentrate, thawed

1 pound box powdered sugar

1 teaspoon dried orange peel

- Blend all ingredients together in mixer. Store in refrigerator.

Great on biscuits and hot rolls.

Ambrosia Spread

1 (11 ounce) can mandarin orange sections, drained

1 (8 ounce) container soft cream cheese with pineapple, softened

¼ cup flaked coconut, toasted

¼ cup slivered almonds, chopped and toasted

- Chop orange sections; set aside.
- Combine cheese, coconut and almonds, blending well. Gently fold in orange sections. Refrigerate.
- Spread on date nut bread, banana bread, etc.

This can also be used as a dip for fruits.

Strawberry Butter

1 (10 ounce) package frozen strawberries, undrained

1 cup unsalted butter, softened

1 cup powdered sugar

Breakfast breads

- Place all ingredients in a food processor or mixer and process until well mixed.

Strawberry butter is delicious on biscuits, muffins or breads.

A Better Scramble

1 (10½ ounce) can
   cheddar cheese soup

8 eggs, lightly beaten

2 tablespoons margarine

Snipped chives

• Pour soup into a bowl and stir until smooth.

• Add the eggs and a little bit of pepper, mixing well.

• In a skillet, melt the margarine. Pour in egg mixture and scramble over low heat until set.

• Sprinkle with chives.

Breakfast Wake Up

12 eggs

2 (7 ounce) cans chopped
   green chilies

2 (16 ounce) packages
   shredded cheddar
   cheese

Salsa, optional

• Drain green chilies, saving juice.

• In a separate bowl, beat eggs with the juice of the green chilies; add a little salt and pepper.

• Spray a 9 x 13-inch pan and spread ½ the cheese on bottom of pan and layer the chilies over this. Top with the remaining cheese.

• Pour eggs over the top and bake uncovered at 350° for 45 minutes.

Cheesy Scrambled Eggs

2 tablespoons margarine

8 eggs

1 (4 ounce) can chopped
   green chilies

½ cup grated cheddar
   cheese

• Melt margarine in a skillet.

• Beat remaining ingredients well, adding a little salt and black pepper; pour into skillet.

• Cook and stir until set.

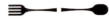

Creamed Eggs

½ stick margarine

4 level tablespoons flour

2 cups milk

6 hard-boiled eggs, sliced

- Melt margarine in skillet; stir in flour. Add milk.
- Cook over medium heat, stirring constantly until sauce is thickened.
- Gently fold in egg slices.

  Serve over six slices toasted bread.

Baked Eggs

4 eggs

4 tablespoons cream, divided

4 tablespoons cracker crumbs, divided

4 tablespoons shredded cheddar cheese, divided

- Grease 4 muffin cups and place egg in each.
- Add 1 tablespoon each of cream, crumbs and cheese for each egg. Sprinkle with a little salt and pepper.
- Bake at 325° for 12 to 20 minutes until eggs are set.

  As many eggs as required may be prepared at the same time.

Mexican Eggs

4 corn tortillas

4 eggs

1 cup green chili salsa

4 ounces grated longhorn cheese

- Dip tortillas in skillet in heated oil and remove quickly. Set tortillas on baking pan to keep warm.
- In skillet, fry eggs in a little butter until the whites are set. Place a fried egg on each tortilla.
- Heat salsa and spoon over each egg. Sprinkle grated cheese on top.
- Place baking pan under broiler just until cheese melts. Serve hot.

Breakfast Tacos

4 eggs

4 flour tortillas

1 cup chopped, cooked ham

1 cup grated cheddar cheese

- Scramble eggs in skillet.
- Lay tortillas flat and spoon eggs over the 4 tortillas.
- Sprinkle with ham and cheese. Roll up to enclose filling.
- Place tacos in a microwave safe dish. Microwave for about 30 seconds or until cheese is melted. Serve immediately.

Glazed Bacon

1 pound bacon

⅓ cup packed brown sugar

1 teaspoon flour

½ cup finely chopped pecans

- Arrange bacon slices close together, but not overlapping, on a wire rack over a drip pan.
- In a bowl, combine the brown sugar, flour and pecans; sprinkle evenly over the bacon.
- Bake at 350° for about 30 minutes. Drain on paper towels.

Pecan Waffles

2 cups self-rising flour

½ cup oil

½ cup milk

⅔ cup finely chopped pecans

- Preheat waffle iron.
- In a bowl, combine flour, oil and milk. Beat until well mixed.
- Stir in chopped pecans.
- Pour approximately ¾ cup of batter into a hot waffle iron and bake until browned and crispy.

Waffle Flash

2 eggs
1 cup milk
½ teaspoon vanilla
8 slices stale bread

- Heat waffle iron according to directions.
- Beat eggs and slowly add milk and vanilla; beat well.
- Remove crust from bread and butter both sides of bread.
- When waffle iron is ready, dip bread in egg mixture and place in waffle iron. Close lid. Grill until lightly brown. Serve with syrup.

Light and Crispy Waffles

2 cups biscuit mix
1 egg
½ cup oil
1⅓ cups club soda

- Preheat waffle iron.
- Combine all ingredients in a mixing bowl and stir by hand.
- Pour just enough batter to cover waffle iron.

To have waffles for a "company weekend", make up all waffles in advance. Freeze separately on cookie sheet, place in large baggies. To heat, warm at 350° for about 10 minutes.

Praline Toast

1 stick butter, softened
1 cup packed brown sugar
⅓ cup finely chopped pecans
Bread slices

- Combine butter, sugar and pecans.
- Spread on bread slices.
- Toast in broiler until brown and bubbly.

French Toast

4 eggs

1 cup whipping cream

2 thick slices bread, cut into 3 strips

Powdered sugar

- Place a little oil in a skillet. Beat together eggs, cream and a pinch of salt.
- Dip bread into batter allowing batter to soak in.
- Fry bread in skillet until brown; turn and fry on the other side.
- Transfer to cookie sheet. Bake at 325° for about 4 minutes or until puffed. Sprinkle with powdered sugar.

Cinnamon Toast

⅔ cup sugar

1 heaping tablespoon cinnamon

Bread

Margarine, softened

- Make cinnamon sugar by mixing sugar with cinnamon. Place in large salt or sugar shaker.
- Place bread on cookie sheet and toast top by broiling in oven until light brown.
- Remove cookie sheet and spread soft margarine on the toasted side. Sprinkle with cinnamon mixture.
- Return to oven and broil until tops are bubbly. Watch closely because sugar burns easily.

Sunrise Tacos

4 eggs, scrambled

½ cup grated cheddar cheese

½ cup salsa

2 flour tortillas

- For each taco, spread ½ scrambled eggs, ¼ cup cheese and ¼ cup salsa on the tortilla and roll up.

Bacon and Egg Burrito

2 slices bacon, cooked, chopped

2 eggs, scrambled

¼ cup shredded cheddar cheese

1 flour tortilla

- Sprinkle bacon, eggs and cheese in the middle of a tortilla. (Also add taco sauce or salsa, if you like.)
- Fold tortilla sides over and place seam side down on a dinner plate.
- Microwave for 30 seconds or just until heated thoroughly.

Jalapeno Pie

1 (4½ ounce) can whole jalapeno peppers

4 eggs

1 pound shredded cheddar cheese

2 tablespoons milk

- Cut peppers in half and remove the seeds. (Use plastic gloves or you will irritate your skin.) Chop the peppers and place them in the bottom of a 9-inch baking dish.
- In a small mixing bowl, beat eggs slightly and stir in cheese and milk.
- Spread egg and cheese mixture evenly over the peppers.
- Bake at 350° for 35 minutes. Let pie stand for 15 minutes before cutting.

Blueberry Coffee Cake

1 (16 ounce) package blueberry muffin mix

⅓ cup sour cream

1 egg

⅔ cup powdered sugar

- Stir together the muffin mix, sour cream, egg and ½ cup water.
- Rinse blueberries and gently fold into batter. Pour into a non-stick vegetable sprayed 7 x 11-inch baking dish.
- Bake at 400° for about 25 minutes.
- Mix powdered sugar and 1 tablespoon water and drizzle over coffee cake.

Sticky Pecan Rolls

1 (12 count) package
brown and serve dinner
rolls

4 tablespoons margarine

⅔ cup packed brown
sugar

24 pecan halves

- Place 1 roll in each of 12 well greased muffin cups.
- Cut an X in top of each roll.
- Combine the sugar and margarine together and melt, mixing well. Spoon mixture over rolls.
- Tuck two pecan halves in cut on each roll. Bake at 350° for 50 minutes or until slightly brown.

Corned Beef Hash Bake

2 (15 ounce) cans corned
beef hash, slightly
warmed

Margarine

6-8 eggs

⅓ cup half-and-half

- Spread corned beef hash in a greased 9 x 13-inch pan. Pat down with the back of a spoon and make 6 to 8 deep hollows in the hash large enough to accommodate an egg.
- Fill hollows with tiny dab of margarine.
- Pour eggs into each hollow and cover the eggs with a tablespoon or so of the cream.
- Bake uncovered at 350° for 15 to 20 minutes or until eggs are set as desired. Divide into squares to serve.

Dog Gones

1 (10 count) can biscuits
1 cup shortening
1 cup sugar
1 teaspoon cinnamon

• Remove biscuits from can and put on piece of wax paper.
• Cut each biscuit into 4 pieces.
• Heat shortening in skillet and drop biscuits in hot oil a few pieces at a time until golden brown. Remove and place on paper towels to drain.
• Dip in the mixture of sugar and cinnamon. Serve warm.

Cheese Enchiladas

1 dozen corn tortillas
1 (8 ounce) package shredded cheddar cheese
½ cup chopped onion
2 (10 ounce) cans enchilada sauce

• Wrap tortillas in a slightly damp paper towel. Put between two salad plates and microwave on high for 45 seconds.
• Place ⅓ cup cheese and a sprinkle of onions on each tortilla; roll up. Place seam side down in a 9 x 13-baking dish. Repeat with remaining tortillas.
• Pour enchilada sauce over enchiladas. Sprinkle with remaining cheese and onions.
• Cover and microwave on medium high for 5 to 6 minutes.

Brunch Pineapple Slices

1 cup cooked ground ham
1 teaspoon mustard
2 tablespoons mayonnaise
5 slices pineapple, drained

• Combine ham, mustard and mayonnaise; mixing well.
• Spread on pineapple slices.
• Bake in an ungreased baking pan at 375° for about 15 minutes or until heated thoroughly.

Chili Rellenos

2 (7 ounce) cans chopped green chilies

1 (16 ounce) package shredded monterey jack cheese

4 eggs, beaten

½ cup milk

- In a 7 x 11-inch baking dish, layer half the green chilies, half the cheese, then the remaining green chilies and cheese.

- Combine the eggs, milk and a little salt and pepper in a small bowl; mix well.

- Pour over the layers of cheese and green chilies.

- Bake uncovered at 350° for 30 minutes or until light brown and set. Cool for 5 minutes before cutting into squares.

Spiced Pears

1 (15 ounce) can pear halves

⅓ cup packed brown sugar

¾ teaspoon ground nutmeg

¾ teaspoon ground cinnamon

- Drain pears, reserving syrup. Set pears aside.

- Place syrup, brown sugar, nutmeg and cinnamon in a saucepan and bring to a boil. Reduce heat and simmer uncovered for 5 to 8 minutes stirring frequently.

- Add pears and simmer 5 minutes longer or until heated thoroughly.

Melon Boats

2 cantaloupes, chilled

4 cups red and green
seedless grapes, chilled

1 cup mayonnaise

⅓ cup frozen
concentrated orange
juice, undiluted

- Prepare each melon in 6 lengthwise
  sections, removing seeds and peel.
  Place on separate salad plates on
  lettuce leaves.

- Heap grapes over and around the
  cantaloupe slices.

- Combine mayonnaise and juice
  concentrate; mixing well.
  Ladle over fruit.

Apricot Casserole

4 (15 ounce) cans apricot
halves, drained

1 (16 ounce) box light
brown sugar, divided

2 cups Ritz cracker
crumbs, divided

1 stick margarine, sliced

- Grease a 9 x 13-inch baking dish and
  line bottom with 2 cans of drained
  apricots.

- Sprinkle half the brown sugar and half
  the cracker crumbs over apricots. Dot
  with half the margarine.

- Repeat layers.

- Bake at 300° for 1 hour.

Apricot Bake

2 (15 ounce) cans apricot
halves, drained

¾ cup packed brown
sugar

1 cup Ritz cracker
crumbs

1 stick margarine, melted

- Butter a 2-quart casserole and layer
  apricots, sugar and cracker crumbs
  until all ingredients are used.

- Melt margarine and pour over casserole.

- Bake at 325° for 35 minutes or until
  cracker crumbs are slightly brown.
  Serve hot or room temperature.

Treasure-Filled Apples

6 tart apples

½ cup sugar

¼ cup cinnamon candies

¼ teaspoon ground
cinnamon

- Cut tops off apples and set tops aside. Core apples to within ½-inch of bottom.
- Place in a greased 8-inch baking dish.
- In a bowl, combine sugar, candies and cinnamon; spoon 2 tablespoons into each apple. Replace the tops.
- Spoon any remaining sugar mixture over the apples.
- Bake, uncovered, at 350° for 30 to 35 minutes or until apples are tender, basting occasionally.

Peachy Fruit Dip

1 (15 ounce) can sliced
peaches, drained

½ cup marshmallow cream

1 (3 ounce) package
cream cheese, cubed

⅛ teaspoon ground nutmeg

- In a blender or food processor, combine all ingredients. Serve with assorted fresh fruit.

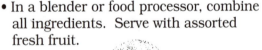

Gingered Cream Spread

1 (8 ounce) package
cream cheese, softened

1 stick unsalted
margarine, softened

2 tablespoons milk

3 tablespoon finely
chopped crystallized
ginger

- Combine all ingredients in mixer. Beat until creamy.
- Spread on your favorite fruit or nut breads.

Bacon Cheese Stromboli

1 (10 ounce) tube refrigerated pizza dough

¾ cup shredded cheddar cheese

¾ cup shredded mozzarella cheese

6 bacon strips, cooked and crumbled

- On an ungreased baking sheet, roll the dough into a 12-inch circle.
- On one half of the dough, sprinkle cheeses and bacon to within ½-inch of edge.
- Fold dough over filling; pinch edges to seal.
- Bake at 400° for about 10 minutes or until golden. Serve with salsa.

Cut in pie slices.

Notes:

_____

_____

_____

_____

_____

_____

_____

_____

_____

_____

_____

_____

_____

_____

_____

_____

_____

_____

SOUPS, SALADS & SANDWICHES

Spicy Tomato Soup

2 (10 ounce) cans tomato
soup

1 (16 ounce) can Mexican
stewed tomatoes

Sour cream

½ pound bacon, fried,
drained, crumbled

- In a saucepan, combine soup and
stewed tomatoes and heat.

- To serve, place a dollop of sour cream
on each bowl of soup and sprinkle
crumbled bacon over sour cream.

Navy Bean Soup

3 cans navy beans,
undrained

1 cup chopped ham

1 large onion, chopped

½ teaspoon garlic powder

- In large saucepan, combine beans, ham,
onion and garlic powder.

- Add 1 cup water and bring to a boil.
Simmer until onion is tender crisp.

Serve hot with cornbread.

Turkey Soup

1 (10½ ounce) can cream
of celery soup

1 (10½ ounce) can cream
of chicken soup

2 (10½ ounce) cans milk
or cream

1 cup finely diced leftover
turkey

- Combine all ingredients in a large
saucepan.

- Serve hot.

Swiss Vegetable Soup

1 (1.5 ounce) package Knorr Swiss vegetable soup mix

3 cups water

1 cup half-and-half

1½ cups shredded Swiss cheese

• Combine soup mix and water in a saucepan. Bring to boiling.

• Lower heat and simmer about 10 minutes.

• Add half-and-half and cheese; serve hot.

Chili Soup Warmer

1 (10½ ounce) can tomato bisque soup

1 (10 ounce) can chili

1 (10½ ounce) can fiesta chili beef soup

1 (15 ounce) can chicken broth

• In a saucepan combine all soups and broth. Depending on how thick you want the soup you can add 1 can of water.

• Heat and serve hot with crackers.

Supper Gumbo

1 (10½ ounce) can condensed pepper pot soup

1 (10½ ounce) can condensed chicken gumbo soup

1 (6 ounce) can white flaked crabmeat

1 (6 ounce) can tiny shrimp

• Combine all ingredients and include 1½ soup cans water. (You might want to add a ¼ teaspoon salt.)

• Cover and simmer for 15 minutes.

Bacon Potato Soup

2 (14 ounce) cans
   chicken broth
   seasoned with garlic

2 potatoes, peeled, cubed

1 onion finely chopped

6 strips bacon, cooked,
   crumbled

- In a large saucepan, combine broth, potatoes and onion. Bring to a boil; reduce heat to medium high and boil about 10 minutes or until potatoes are tender.
- Season with pepper.
- Ladle into bowls and sprinkle with crumbled bacon.

Cheesy Chicken Soup

1 (10½ ounce) can fiesta
   nacho cheese soup

1 (10½ ounce) can cream
   of chicken soup

1 soup can milk

1 chicken bouillon cube
   or 1 teaspoon bouillon
   granules

- Mix all ingredients in saucepan and stir until smooth. Serve hot.

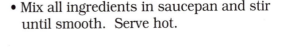

Tomato French Onion Soup

1 (10½ ounce) can tomato
   bisque soup

2 (10½ ounce) cans
   French onion soup

Grated parmesan cheese

Croutons

- In saucepan combine soups and 2 soup cans of water. Heat thoroughly.
- Serve in bowls topped with croutons and a sprinkle of cheese.

Speedy Taco Soup

1 (12 ounce) can chicken, undrained

1 (14 ounce) can chicken broth

1 (16 ounce) jar mild thick and chunky salsa

1 (15 ounce) can ranch-style beans

- In large saucepan combine chicken, broth, salsa and beans. A 15-ounce can of whole kernel corn could also be added.
- Bring to a boil, reduce heat and simmer 15 minutes.

Crab Soup

1 package dry onion soup mix

1 (6 ounce) can crabmeat, including liquid

1 (8 ounce) carton whipping cream

½ cup white wine

- Dissolve soup mix in 2 cups water.
- Add crabmeat, crab liquid and whipping cream. Season with salt and pepper.
- Heat, but not to the boiling stage, and simmer for 20 minutes.
- Stir in wine; heat. Serve warm.

Peanut Soup

2 (10½ ounce) cans cream of chicken soup

2 soup cans milk

1¼ cups crunchy peanut butter

½ teaspoon celery salt

- In a saucepan on medium heat, blend together the soup and milk.
- Stir in peanut butter and celery salt and heat until well blended.

Clam Chowder

1 (10½ ounce) can New
  England clam chowder
1 (10½ ounce) can cream
  of celery soup
1 (10½ ounce) can cream
  of potato soup
½ cup whole milk

• Combine all ingredients in saucepan.
• Heat and stir.

Asparagus Chiller

1 (10½ ounce) can
  condensed cream of
  asparagus soup
⅔ cup sour cream
½ cup finely chopped
  cucumber
2 tablespoons chopped
  red onion

• Blend soup, sour cream and 1 soup can
  water.
• Add cucumber and onion.
• Chill at least 4 hours and serve in
  chilled bowls.

Squash Soup

2 pounds fresh, yellow
  squash, thinly sliced
1 onion, chopped
1 (14 ounce) can chicken
  broth
1 (8 ounce) carton sour
  cream

• In a saucepan simmer squash and
  onions in the broth until very tender.
• Chill.
• Just before serving, add sour cream and
  a little salt and pepper.
• Serve chilled.

Red and Green Salad

2 (10 ounce) packages
fresh spinach

1 quart fresh
strawberries, halved

½ cup slivered almonds,
toasted

Poppy seed dressing

- Tear spinach into smaller pieces and add the strawberries and almonds.
- Refrigerate until ready to serve.
- Toss with poppy seed dressing.

Romaine Salad

1 large head romaine
lettuce

2 tablespoons sesame
seeds, toasted

6 strips bacon, fried,
crumbled

½ cup grated Swiss
cheese

- Wash and dry lettuce. Tear into bite-size pieces.
- When ready to serve, sprinkle sesame seeds, bacon and cheese over lettuce and toss with a creamy Italian dressing.

Salad Surprise

1 (10 ounce) bag fresh
spinach, washed,
stemmed

1 pint fresh strawberries,
stemmed, halved

1 large banana, sliced

⅔ cup chopped walnuts

- Place all salad ingredients in a large bowl.
- When ready to serve, toss with poppy seed dressing.

Strawberry Spinach Salad

1 (10 ounce) package
   fresh spinach, washed,
   stemmed

1 small jicama, peeled,
   julienned

1 pint fresh strawberries,
   stemmed, halved

2½ cups fresh bean
   sprouts

• Combine spinach, jicama, strawberries and bean sprouts in a large bowl.

• Toss with poppy seed dressing just before serving.

Mandarin Salad

1 head red tipped lettuce

2 (11 ounce) cans
   mandarin oranges,
   drained

2 avocadoes, peeled,
   diced

1 small red onion, sliced

• Combine all ingredients.

• When ready to serve, toss with a poppy seed dressing.

Crunchy Salad

¼ cup sesame seeds

½ cup sunflower seeds

½ cup almonds

1 head red leaf lettuce

• Toast the sesame seeds, sunflower seeds and almonds in a 300° oven for about 15 minutes or until lightly browned.

• Tear lettuce into bite-size pieces and add seed mixture.

• Toss with creamy Italian dressing.

Oriental Spinach Salad

1 (10 ounce) package
fresh spinach

1 (16 ounce) can bean
sprouts, drained

8 slices bacon, cooked
crisp

1 (11 ounce) can water
chestnuts, chopped

- Combine spinach and bean sprouts.
- When ready to serve add the crumbled bacon and toss with a vinaigrette salad dressing made from 3 parts olive oil and 1 part red wine vinegar.

Swiss Salad

1 large head romaine
lettuce

1 bunch fresh green
onions and tops,
chopped

1 (8 ounce) package of
shredded Swiss cheese

½ cup toasted sunflower
seeds

- Tear the lettuce into bite-size pieces.
- Add onions, cheese, sunflower seeds and toss.
- Serve with a vinaigrette dressing.

Vinaigrette for Swiss Salad

⅔ cup oil

⅓ cup red wine vinegar

1 tablespoon seasoned
salt

- Mix all ingredients and refrigerate.

Spinach Bacon Salad

1 (10 ounce) package
  fresh spinach

3 hardcooked eggs,
  chopped

8 mushroom caps, sliced

1 (11 ounce) can water
  chestnuts, chopped

• Mix all ingredients together and serve with hot bacon dressing.

Hot Bacon Dressing for Spinach Bacon Salad

½ pound bacon, chopped

1 cup sugar

1⅓ cups white vinegar

5 teaspoons corn starch

• To make dressing fry the bacon until crisp. Remove bacon to drain and leave bacon drippings in skillet.

• Add the sugar and vinegar to the skillet, stirring well. Add one cup water and bring to a boil.

• Mix corn starch with ⅔ cup water and stir until dissolved. Pour corn starch mixture into the skillet with the dressing. Return to a boil; simmer for 5 minutes.

• Remove from heat and toss salad with warm bacon dressing.

Orange Almond Salad

1 head green leaf lettuce

4 slices bacon, fried,
  crumbled

⅓ cup slivered almonds,
  toasted

1 (11 ounce) can
  mandarin oranges,
  drained, chilled

• Combine all ingredients in a salad bowl.

• When ready to serve toss with a vinaigrette dressing.

Spinach Orange Salad

1 (10 ounce) package
  spinach, stems
  removed

2 (10 ounce) cans
  mandarin oranges,
  drained

⅓ small jicama, peeled,
  julienned

⅓ cup slivered almonds,
  toasted

• In a large bowl, combine spinach,
  oranges, jicama and almonds.

• Toss with vinaigrette dressing.

Spinach Salad Oriental

1 (10 ounce) package
  fresh spinach

2 hardboiled eggs, sliced

1 (14 ounce) can bean
  sprouts, drained

1 (8 ounce) can water
  chestnuts, chopped

• Combine all four ingredients. Top with
  dressing.

Dressing for Spinach Salad Oriental

¾ cup olive oil

⅓ cup sugar

¼ cup ketchup

3 tablespoons red wine
  vinegar

• Combine all ingredients mixing well.

• You do not need all of this dressing for
  this salad. Refrigerate remaining salad
  dressing.

Red Hot Onions

3 large purple onions
2 tablespoons Tabasco
3 tablespoons olive oil
3 tablespoons red wine
  vinegar

- Slice onions thinly. Pour a cup of boiling water over onions and let stand 1 minute; drain.
- Mix Tabasco, oil and vinegar and pour over onion rings in a shallow bowl with a lid.
- Refrigerate and let stand at least 3 hours.
- Drain to serve.

Good with barbecue.

Special Spinach Salad

1 (10 ounce) package
  fresh spinach
1 (16 ounce) can bean
  sprouts, drained
8 slices bacon, cooked
  crisp
1 (11 ounce) can water
  chestnuts, chopped

- Combine spinach and bean sprouts.
- When ready to serve add the crumbled bacon and toss with a vinaigrette salad dressing made from 3 parts olive oil and 1 part red wine vinegar.

Red Cabbage Slaw

1 large head red cabbage
2 onions, chopped
½ cup cole slaw dressing
½ cup French dressing

- Slice cabbage and combine with onions.
- Combine dressing and toss with cabbage and onions.
- Refrigerate.

Hawaiian Slaw

2 envelopes unflavored gelatin

3 cups orange juice, divided

1 (8 ounce) can crushed pineapple, undrained

2 cups finely shredded cabbage

- Sprinkle gelatin over 1 cup orange juice in a saucepan. Heat until gelatin is dissolved.
- Stir in remaining orange juice and chill until slightly thickened.
- Fold in pineapple and cabbage; blend well.
- Pour into a 8 x 8-inch dish and refrigerate until set.

Deviled Eggs

6 hardcooked eggs

2 tablespoons sweet pickle relish

3 tablespoons mayonnaise

½ teaspoon mustard

- Peel eggs and cut in half lengthwise. Take yolks out and mash with fork.
- Add relish, mayonnaise and mustard to yolks. Place this yolk mixture back into the egg white halves.
- Sprinkle with paprika, if you like.

Broccoli and Pepperoni Salad

1 pound bunch broccoli

½ pound fresh mushrooms, sliced

6 ounces Swiss cheese, diced

1 (3 ounce) package sliced pepperoni, chopped

- Cut off broccoli flowerets; combine broccoli, mushrooms, cheese, pepperoni.
- Toss with an Italian dressing.
- Refrigerate at least 8 hours before serving.

Bean and Onion Salad

1 (15 ounce) can whole green beans

1 (15 ounce) can yellow wax beans

½ cup finely chopped red onion

¼ cup slivered almonds

• Combine all ingredients.

Dressing for Bean and Onion Salad

¼ cup oil

1 tablespoon white vinegar

1 teaspoon sugar

2 teaspoons dijon mustard

• Combine all ingredients adding ½ teaspoon salt and ½ teaspoon black pepper.

• Pour over bean and onion salad.

• Refrigerate at least 1 hour before serving.

Cashew Pea Salad

1 (16 ounce) package frozen green peas, thawed

¼ cup diced celery

1 bunch fresh green onions, chopped (tops too)

1 cup chopped cashews

• Combine the peas, celery, onions and cashews.

• Toss with ½ cup mayonnaise seasoned with ½ teaspoon seasoned salt and black pepper.

Marinated Brussel Sprout Medley

2 (10 ounce) boxes frozen brussel sprouts

1 cup Italian dressing

1 cup chopped green bell pepper

½ cup chopped onion

- Pierce box of brussel sprouts and cook in microwave for 7 minutes.
- Mix together the Italian dressing, bell pepper and onion.
- Pour over brussel sprouts and marinate for at least 24 hours.
- Drain to serve.

Pasta Salad

1 (16 ounce) package corkscrew pasta

1 (16 ounce) package frozen broccoli-cauliflower combination

1 (8 ounce) package mozzarella cheese, cut in small chunks

1 (8 ounce) bottle Catalina salad dressing

- Cook pasta according to package directions. Drain and cool.
- Cook vegetables in microwave according to package directions. Drain and cool.
- In a large bowl, combine pasta, vegetables and cheese chunks.
- Toss with catalina dressing. Refrigerate several hours before serving.

Marinated Brussel Sprouts

2 (10 ounce) packages brussel sprouts, cooked

½ cup salad oil

¼ cup white wine vinegar

¼ cup sugar

- Mix all ingredients and marinate overnight.
- Serve cold.

Sunny Corn Salad

2 (15 ounce) cans
  mexicorn, drained

1 red bell pepper,
  chopped

1 onion, chopped

Italian salad dressing

• Combine corn, pepper and onion.

• Pour about 1 cup of the salad dressing over vegetables and chill several hours.

• Refrigerate. Drain to serve.

Sour Cream Potato Salad

12 medium red potatoes,
  unpeeled

1¼ cups mayonnaise

1 cup sour cream

1 cup fresh green onions
  and tops, chopped

• Boil red potatoes until done, about 20 minutes. Slice potatoes.

• Combine mayonnaise, sour cream and 1 teaspoon salt.

• When potatoes are cool toss with sour cream mixture (1 tablespoon horseradish can be added if you like horseradish). Add green onion.

Carrot Salad

3 cups finely grated
  carrots

1 (8 ounce) can crushed
  pineapple, drained

4 tablespoons coconut

1 tablespoon sugar

• Combine all ingredients. Toss with ⅓ cup mayonnaise, mixing well.

• Refrigerate.

Cucumber Salad

1 (3 ounce) package lime gelatin

2 medium cucumbers

1 tablespoon minced onion

½ cup mayonnaise, ½ cup sour cream

- Dissolve gelatin in ¾ cup boiling water; mixing well. Bring to room temperature.
- Slice cucumber in half and remove seeds. Grate cucumber and add to cooled gelatin along with the onion, mayonnaise and sour cream.
- Pour into a square dish.
- Refrigerate until set.

Chilled Cucumbers

2 cucumbers, peeled, sliced

½ onion, sliced

¼ cup vinegar

⅓ cup sugar

- Place cucumbers and onion in a bowl with a lid.
- Combine vinegar and sugar. Pour over cucumbers and onions.
- Cover and chill for 2 to 3 hours before serving.

Marinated Cucumbers

⅓ cup vinegar

2 tablespoons sugar

1 teaspoon dried dill weed

3 cucumbers, peeled, sliced

- Combine the vinegar, sugar, 1 teaspoon salt, dill weed and about ¼ teaspoon black pepper. Pour over the cucumbers.
- Refrigerate one hour before serving.

  You could add onion to the cucumbers if you like.

115

Cucumber Slices

3 cucumbers, peeled

2 (3 ounce) packages
   cream cheese, softened

¼ cup stuffed green
   olives, chopped

½ teaspoon seasoned salt

- Half cucumbers lengthwise and scoop out seeds.
- Beat cream cheese with mixer, until creamy. Add olives and seasoned salt.
- Fill hollows with cream cheese mixture, press halves together and wrap tightly in plastic wrap; chill.
- Cut crosswise in ⅓-inch slices to serve.

Grape Salad

1 pound seedless green
   grapes, halved

½ cup chopped pecans

⅔ cup shredded cheddar
   cheese

1 (15 ounce) can
   pineapple tidbits,
   drained

- Combine grapes, pecans, cheese and pineapple. Fold in about ½ cup of mayonnaise.
- Serve on lettuce leaves.

Marinated Onion Rings

2 pounds of white onion,
   thinly sliced

1 cup sugar

2 cups white vinegar

½ teaspoon salt

- Cover onions with boiling water and let stand for five minutes. Drain.
- Combine sugar, vinegar and salt; pour over onion.
- Refrigerate.

Broccoli Cheese Salad

4 cups broccoli, cut into
bit size pieces

1 red onion, chopped

½ pound cheddar cheese,
cubed

6 slices bacon, cooked,
crumbled

- Combine all ingredients. (You could substitute mozzarella cheese if you like.)
- Toss with broccoli dressing.

Broccoli Dressing

1 cup mayonnaise

¼ cup sugar

2 tablespoons vinegar

- Mix well and pour over broccoli cheese salad.

Green Beans With Tomatoes

2 pounds frozen cut
green beans

4 tomatoes, chopped,
drained

1 bunch green onions,
chopped

1 cup Italian salad
dressing

- Place beans in a saucepan and cover with water; bring to a boil. Cook uncovered for 8 to 10 minutes or until tender crisp; drain, chill.
- Add the tomatoes, green onions and salad dressing; toss to coat.

Green and White Salad

1 (16 ounce) package frozen green peas, thawed, uncooked

1 head cauliflower, cut into bite-size pieces

1 (8 ounce) carton sour cream

1 envelope dry ranch-style salad dressing

• In a large bowl, combine the peas and cauliflower.

• Combine sour cream and salad dressing. Toss with the vegetables.

• Refrigerate.

Salad is even better if you add half of a purple onion, chopped.

Color Coded Salad

1 (16 ounce) package tri-colored macaroni, cooked, drained

1 red bell pepper, julienned

1 cup chopped zucchini

1 cup broccoli flowerets

• Combine all ingredients.

• Toss with about 1 cup of Caesar salad dressing.

• Refrigerate.

Snicker Salad

6 large delicious apples, unpeeled, chopped

6 (2 ounce) Snicker candy bars, chopped

½ cup chopped pecans, optional

1 (12 ounce) carton whipped topping

• In a large bowl, combine apples, candy bars and pecans; mixing well.

• Fold in whipped topping.

• Refrigerate.

It is better served the same day.

Cool Apricot Salad

1 (15 ounce) can crushed pineapple, undrained

1 (6 ounce) package apricot gelatin

2 cups buttermilk

1 (12 ounce) carton whipped topping

- Bring pineapple and juice to a boil. Add the gelatin and stir until well dissolved. Cool completely.
- When mixture begins to thicken, add buttermilk and fold in the whipped topping.
- Pour into a 9 x 13-inch glass dish and refrigerate.
- Cut into squares and serve.

Pineapple Ginger Salad

1 (20 ounce) can pineapple tidbits, reserve juice

1 (6 ounce) package lime gelatin

1 cup ginger ale

¼ teaspoon ground ginger

- Heat ½ cup pineapple juice (if not enough juice, add water to make ½ cup). Pour boiling juice over gelatin, mixing well.
- Add ginger ale and ginger. Chill until slightly thickened.
- Fold in pineapple tidbits and spoon into a 7 x 11-inch shallow dish.
- Refrigerate.

Coca Cola Salad

1 (6 ounce) package cherry gelatin

1 (10 ounce) bottle maraschino cherries, drained

1 cup Coca-Cola

1 cup chopped pecans

- Add gelatin in ¾ cup boiling water.
- Chop cherries into four slices each. Add cherries, Coca-Cola and pecans.
- Pour into an 8-cup gelatin mold.
- Refrigerate until firm.

Salad Berry Dream

1 (6 ounce) package
blackberry gelatin

1 (15 ounce) can crushed
pineapple, juice
reserved

1 (15 ounce) can
blueberries, drained

Whipped topping, optional

- Add enough water to the pineapple juice to make 2 cups. Put in saucepan and bring to a boil. Pour hot liquid over the gelatin and mix until dissolved.
- Chill until this mixture begins to thicken. Stir in pineapple and blueberries.
- Pour into a 7 x 11-inch dish. Refrigerate.

Topping for Salad Berry Dream

1 (8 ounce) package
cream cheese, softened

1 (8 ounce) carton sour
cream

½ cup sugar

½ cup chopped pecans

- In mixer beat together the cream cheese, sour cream and sugar. Beat until smooth and fluffy.
- Spoon over congealed salad.
- Sprinkle pecans over congealed salad.
- Refrigerate.

Cherry Salad

1 (6 ounce) box cherry
gelatin

1 (8 ounce) package
cream cheese, softened

1 (20 ounce) can cherry
pie filling

1 (15 ounce) can crushed
pineapple, undrained

- Dissolve gelatin with ¾ cup of boiling water.
- With electric mixer beat in the cream cheese, beating very slowly at first. Fold in pie filling and crushed pineapple.
- Pour into a 9 x 13-inch casserole dish. Refrigerate.

Mincemeat Mold

1 (6 ounce) package
cherry gelatin

1 cup prepared
mincemeat

1 rib celery, chopped

⅔ cup chopped pecans

- Dissolve the gelatin in ¾ cup of boiling water.
- Fold in mincemeat, celery and chopped pecans.
- Pour into an 8-inch mold and refrigerate.

Frozen Cranberry Salad

1 (15 ounce) can whole
cranberry sauce

1 (15 ounce) can crushed
pineapple, undrained

1 (8 ounce) carton sour
cream

Lettuce leaves

- Mix all ingredients together and freeze in the cranberry can and another can of equal size.
- When ready to serve, cut upper end of the can out and push salad out.
- Slice and serve on a lettuce leaf.

Watergate Salad

1 (20 ounce) can crushed
pineapple, undrained

2 (3.4 ounce) packages
pistachio instant
pudding mix

¾ cup chopped pecans

1 (12 ounce) carton
whipped topping

- Mix pineapple with instant pudding mix until slightly thickened; add pecans.
- When mixed well, fold in whipped topping.
- Pour into a pretty crystal bowl and refrigerate.

One cup of miniature marshmallows may be added.

Cashew Salad

1 (6 ounce) package
  lemon gelatin

1 quart vanilla ice cream

1 (15 ounce) can fruit
  cocktail, drained

1¼ cups chopped cashew
  nuts

• Dissolve gelatin in 1-cup boiling water
  and stir in ice cream. Blend until ice
  cream is melted.

• Add fruit cocktail and cashew nuts; mix
  well.

• Pour into an 8 x 11-inch glass dish.
  Refrigerate overnight.

Cranberry Salad

1 (6 ounce) package
  cherry gelatin

1 can whole cranberry
  sauce

1 pint sour cream

¾ cup chopped pecans

• Dissolve gelatin in 1¼ cups of boiling
  water. When well mixed, add cranberry
  sauce.

• Mix well and refrigerate until it begins to
  congeal, then add sour cream and
  pecans, mixing well.

• Pour into a 7 x 11-inch casserole.
  Refrigerate for several hours before
  serving.

Cherry Cranberry Salad

1 (6 ounce) package
  cherry gelatin

1 cup boiling water

1 (20 ounce) can cherry
  pie filling

1 (16 ounce) can whole
  cranberry sauce

• In mixing bowl, combine cherry gelatin
  and boiling water; mixing until gelatin is
  dissolved.

• Mix pie filling and cranberry sauce into
  gelatin.

• Pour into a 7 x 11-inch dish and refrigerate.

Creamy Cranberry Salad

1 (6 ounce) package
cherry gelatin

1 (8 ounce) carton sour
cream

1 (16 ounce) can whole
cranberry sauce

1 (8 ounce) can crushed
pineapple, undrained

• Dissolve gelatin in 1-cup boiling water,
mixing well.

• Stir in remaining ingredients and pour
into a 7 x 11-inch glass dish.

• Refrigerate until firm.

Frozen Cranberry-Pineapple Salad

1 (20 ounce) can crushed
pineapple, drained

2 (16 ounce) cans whole
cranberry sauce

1 (8 ounce) carton sour
cream

¾ cup chopped pecans

• In large bowl, combine all ingredients.

• Pour into a greased loaf pan.

• Freeze several hours before serving.

Luscious Strawberry Salad

1 (6 ounce) package
strawberry gelatin

2 (10 ounce) boxes frozen
strawberries, thawed

3 bananas, sliced

1 (8 ounce) carton sour
cream

• Dissolve gelatin in 1 cup boiling water,
mixing well. Add strawberries and
bananas.

• Pour half mixture in a 9 x 13-inch dish,
leaving all the bananas in the bottom
layer. Chill until firm.

• Spread sour cream over firm gelatin.

• Add remaining gelatin over sour cream.
Refrigerate until firm.

Tropical Mango Salad

2 (15 ounce) cans
mangoes, reserve juice

1 (6 ounce) package
orange gelatin

1 (8 ounce) package
cream cheese, softened

½ (8 ounce) carton
whipped topping

- Place all mango slices on a dinner plate and with a knife and fork, cut slices into bite-size pieces. Place 1½ cups of the mango juice (if not that much juice, add water to make 1½ cups) in a saucepan and bring to boiling point.

- Pour over gelatin in mixer bowl and mix well.

- Add cream cheese and start mixer very slowly. Gradually increase speed until cream cheese is mixed into gelatin. Pour in mango pieces.

- Place in refrigerator until it is lightly congealed. Fold in whipped topping. Pour into a 7 x 11-inch dish. Chill.

Cream Cheese and Mango Salad

2 (15 ounce) cans
mangoes

1 (6 ounce) package
lemon gelatin

2 (8 ounces) cream
cheese, softened

1 (8 ounce) can crushed
pineapple, undrained

- Drain juice from mangoes. Combine juice and enough water to make ¾ cups liquid. Bring to a boil and add gelatin. Stir until well dissolved.

- In mixing bowl, cream together the mangoes and cream cheese. Fold in pineapple.

- Mix into hot gelatin and pour into muffin tins or a mold.

Mango Salad

2 (15 ounce) cans
  mangoes

3 (3 ounce) packages
  lemon gelatin

1 (8 ounce) package
  cream cheese, cubed
  and softened

2 tablespoons lemon
  juice

- Drain mangoes reserving juice. Add water to make 2 cups liquid. Heat to boiling. Dissolve gelatin in juice mixture. Cool.
- Put mixture in a blender and add mangoes, cream cheese and lemon juice. Blend slowly at first until smooth.
- Pour into a 6-cup mold.
- Chill several hours or overnight.

Pineapple Salad

1 (20 ounce) can crushed
  pineapple, undrained

1 (6 ounce) package
  lemon gelatin

1 (8 ounce) package
  cream cheese, softened
  and cubed

1 (8 ounce) carton
  whipped topping,
  thawed

- Heat pineapple to boiling. Pour over gelatin in mixing bowl and stir to dissolve.
- Combine pineapple mixture and cream cheese; whip slowly until well combined.
- Chill until partially set.
- Fold in the whipped topping and pour into an 8-cup mold.

Apple Pineapple Salad

1 (6 ounce) package
lemon gelatin

1 (15 ounce) can
pineapple tidbits,
undrained

1 cup diced apples,
unpeeled

1 cup chopped pecans

• Dissolve gelatin in one cup boiling
water. Add pineapple and place in
refrigerator until slightly thickened.

• Fold in apples and pecans.

• Pour into a solid mold or into a 7 x 11-
inch dish. Chill until firm.

Stained Glass Fruit Salad

2 (20 ounce) cans peach
pie filling

3 bananas, sliced

1 (16 ounce) package
frozen unsweetened
strawberries, drained

1 (20 ounce) can
pineapple tidbits,
drained

• Drain all fruits except peach pie filling.

• Mix all fruits together; chill and place in
a pretty crystal bowl.

• Chill overnight.

*If you like you could use 1 can peach
pie filling and 1 can apricot pie
filling.*

Pineapple Banana Salad

1 (6 ounce) package lime
gelatin

1 (8 ounce) can crushed
pineapple, undrained

½ cup sour cream

1 large banana, sliced

• Dissolve gelatin in 1 cup boiling water;
mixing well. Stir in pineapple.

• Place in refrigerator until mixture begins
to thicken.

• Fold in sour cream and banana and
pour into an 8-inch mold.

*A ½ cup chopped pecans could be
added.*

Orange Glow

1 (6 ounce) package orange gelatin

1 cup finely grated carrots

1 (15 ounce) can crushed pineapple, undrained

¾ cup chopped pecans

- Mix gelatin in 1 cup boiling water; mixing well.
- Add carrots, pineapple and pecans.
- Pour into a 7 x 11-inch glass dish. Refrigerate until congealed.

Orange Salad

1 (3 ounce) package orange gelatin

1 (3 ounce) package lemon gelatin

1 pint orange sherbet

2 (11 ounce) cans mandarin oranges

- Place gelatin in a bowl and pour 1 cup boiling water over gelatin, mixing well.
- Fold in sherbet; stir until well mixed.
- Add oranges and pour into an 8-inch ring mold or 7 x 11-inch dish. Refrigerate.

Glazed Fruit Salad

2 (11 ounce) cans mandarin oranges, drained

1 (15 ounce) can pineapple chunks, drained

3 bananas, sliced

1 (18 ounce) carton creamy glaze for bananas

- In a large bowl combine fruit and glaze.
- Toss to coat fruit.
- Serve immediately.

Grapes, apples or marshmallows could also be added to this salad.

Lime Cherry Salad

1 (6 ounce) package lime gelatin

1 (10 ounce) bottle maraschino cherries, cut in half

1 cup diced apples, unpeeled

1 cup chopped pecans

- Dissolve gelatin in 1½ cups boiling water; mixing well.
- Add the drained cherries and place in refrigerator until slightly congealed.
- Add apples and pecans and pour into a 7 x 11-inch dish. Chill until firm.

Orange Pear Salad

1 (15 ounce) can sliced pears, reserve juice

1 (16 ounce) package orange gelatin

1 (8 ounce) package cream cheese, softened

1 (8 ounce) carton whipped topping

- Drain pears and reserve juice. Boil juice and ½ cup water. Then add gelatin and dissolve. Mix thoroughly and refrigerate until partially set.
- Blend pears and cream cheese in blender. Fold in pear mixture and whipped topping into gelatin mixture. Blend well.
- Pour into a 7 x 11-inch shallow dish.

Applesauce Salad

2 cups applesauce

1 (6 ounce) package lime gelatin

2 (12 ounce) cans lemon lime carbonated drink

1 (8 ounce) can crushed pineapple, drained

- Heat applesauce in a large saucepan.
- Add gelatin to the hot applesauce and stir until dissolved. Add lemon lime drink and pineapple.
- Pour into an 8-inch mold. Refrigerate.

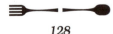

Peaches and Cream

1 (29 ounce) can sliced peaches

1 (6 ounce) package peach gelatin

1 quart vanilla ice cream, softened

1 (11 ounce) can mandarin oranges, drained

- Drain peaches, reserving 1 cup liquid. Cut peach slices into cubes.
- Heat peach liquid and ½ cup water until boiling. Add gelatin and mix well.
- Fold in vanilla ice cream, stirring well.
- Add peaches and mandarin oranges and pour into a mold until set.

Coconut Orange Salad

1 (6 ounce) package orange gelatin

1 pint vanilla ice cream, softened

½ cup coconut

1 (11 ounce) can mandarin oranges, drained

- Dissolve gelatin in 1 cup boiling water. Let cool slightly. Fold in ice cream, coconut and oranges.
- Pour into a 7 x 11-inch dish and refrigerate.

Cinnamon Apple Salad

1 cup cinnamon red hot candies

1 (6 ounce) package cherry gelatin

1 (16 ounce) jar applesauce

1 cup chopped pecans

- Heat cinnamon red hots in 1¼ cups boiling water until candy melts.
- While mixture is still hot, pour over gelatin and mix well. Add applesauce and chopped pecans, mixing well.
- Pour into 7 x 11-inch glass dish and refrigerate until firm. When serving, cut in squares.

Coconut Bananas

4 bananas

4 tablespoons lemon juice

1 (16 ounce) carton sour cream

1¼ cups flaked coconut

- Cut bananas into fourths.
- Place lemon juice, sour cream and coconut in separate bowls.
- Dip bananas into lemon juice, roll in sour cream and then in coconut. Cover thoroughly.
- Place in covered bowl and refrigerate several hours or overnight.

Grapefruit-Avocado Salad

2 (15 ounce) cans grapefruit sections, drained

2 ripe avocados, peeled, sliced

½ cup chopped slivered almonds

Prepared poppy seed dressing

- Combine grapefruit, avocados and almonds.
- Toss with the poppy seed dressing. Serve on a bed of lettuce.

Crunchy Fruit Salad

2 red apples, chopped

⅓ cup sunflower seeds

½ cup green grapes

⅓ cup vanilla yogurt

- In a bowl, combine the apples, sunflower seeds, grapes and yogurt. Stir to coat salad. Refrigerate until serving.

Cranberry Mousse

1 (15 ounce) can jellied cranberry sauce

1 (8 ounce) can crushed pineapple, drained

1 (8 ounce) carton sour cream

1 tablespoon mayonnaise

- In a saucepan place the cranberry sauce and crushed pineapple. Cook until cranberry sauce is liquid.
- Fold in the sour cream and mayonnaise.
- Pour into molds or muffin tins and freeze.

Nutty Cranberry Relish

1 pound fresh cranberries

2¼ cups sugar

1 cup chopped pecans, toasted

1 cup orange marmalade

- Wash and drain cranberries and mix with sugar. Place in 1-quart baking dish. Cover dish and bake at 350° for one hour.
- Add marmalade and pecans to cranberry mixture.
- Mix well and pour into a container. Chill before serving.

Chicken Caesar Salad

4 boneless skinless chicken breasts, grilled

1 (10 ounce) package romaine salad greens

½ cup shredded parmesan cheese

1 cup seasoned croutons

- Cut chicken breasts into strips.
- Combine chicken, salad greens, cheese and croutons in a large bowl.
- When ready to serve, toss with about ¾ cup Caesar Italian dressing.

Ginger Dressing for Fruit Salad

1 cup vanilla yogurt

2 tablespoons honey

1 teaspoon sugar

2 tablespoons finely
  minced, crystallized
  ginger

• Combine all ingredients; mixing well.
  Cover and refrigerate. This may be
  served over any fruit salad.

Mexican Chicken Salad

3-4 boneless skinless
  chicken breasts,
  cooked, cubed

1 (15 ounce) can chick
  peas (garbanzo beans),
  drained

1 red bell pepper, 1 green
  bell pepper, seeded,
  diced

1 cup chopped celery

• Combine all ingredients and serve with
  the following dressing.

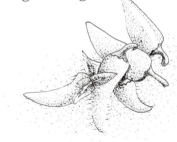

Dressing for Mexican Chicken Salad

1½ cups sour cream

2 tablespoons chili sauce

2 teaspoons ground
  cumin

1 small bunch cilantro,
  finely chopped

• Combine all ingredients for the dressing.
  Add a little salt and black pepper.

• Pour over chicken salad and toss. Chill
  before serving.

Tarragon Chicken Salad

1 cup chopped, toasted pecans

3-4 boneless, skinless chicken breasts, cooked, cubed

1 cup chopped celery

¾ cup peeled chopped cucumbers

- Place pecans in a shallow pan; toast at 300° for 10 minutes.
- Combine the chicken, celery and cucumbers.

Dressing for Tarragon Chicken Salad

⅔ cup mayonnaise

1 tablespoon lemon juice

2 tablespoons tarragon vinegar

1¼ teaspoons crumbled, dried tarragon

- Mix all dressing ingredients together. When ready to serve toss with the chicken mixture, add pecans.

Pear Mousse

2 (15 ounce) cans sliced pears, reserve juice

1 (6 ounce) package lemon gelatin

1 (8 ounce) package cream cheese, softened

1 (8 ounce) carton whipped topping

- Drain pears, reserving juice. Heat juice and add water to make ¾ cup. Heat juice to boiling point. Add gelatin. Mix well and cool.
- Place pears and cream cheese in blender and blend until smooth. Place into a large bowl and fold in cooled but not congealed gelatin mixture and whipped topping. Mix until smooth.
- Pour into individual dessert dishes. Cover with a piece of saran wrap and refrigerate.

To garnish place a slice of kiwi on top of the mousse.

Apple Walnut Chicken Salad

3-4 boneless, skinless
chicken breasts,
cooked, cubed

2 tart green apples,
peeled, chopped

½ cup chopped pitted
dates

1 cup finely chopped
celery

• Mix all ingredients together.
• Toss with dressing.

Dressing

½ cup chopped, toasted
walnuts

⅓ cup sour cream

⅓ cup mayonnaise

1 tablespoon lemon juice

• Toast walnuts at 300° for 10 minutes.
• Mix together sour cream, mayonnaise
and lemon juice.
• Mix with walnuts.
• Pour over chicken salad and toss.
Refrigerate.

Broccoli Chicken Salad

3-4 boneless, skinless
chicken breasts,
cooked, cubed

2 cups fresh broccoli
flowerets

1 sweet red bell pepper,
seeded, chopped

1 cup chopped celery

• Combine chicken, broccoli, bell pepper
and celery.
• Toss with a honey mustard dressing.
Refrigerate.

Black Bean Chicken Salad

3-4 boneless, skinless chicken breasts, cooked, cubed

1 (15 ounce) can black beans, drained

1 bunch green onions, chopped

1 cup chopped celery

• Blend all ingredients together and toss with the following dressing.

Cumin Vinaigrette

¾ cup virgin olive oil

¼ cup lemon juice

2 teaspoons dijon mustard

2 teaspoons ground cumin

• Combine all ingredients together.

• Toss with black bean and chicken salad. Refrigerate.

Derby Chicken Salad

3-4 boneless, skinless chicken breasts, cooked, cubed

¼ pound bacon, cooked, crumbled

2 avocados, peeled, diced

2 tomatoes, diced, drained

• Combine all ingredients.

• When ready to serve pour Italian salad dressing over salad and toss. Refrigerate.

Savory Chicken Salad

4 boneless, skinless chicken breasts, cooked

1 cup chopped celery

1 red bell pepper, seeded, chopped

⅔ cup slivered almonds, toasted

- Slice chicken breasts into long thin strips.
- Combine chicken, celery, bell pepper and almonds. Toss and refrigerate.

For dressing use a flavored mayonnaise (½ cup mayonnaise with 1 tablespoon lemon juice).

Simply Sweet Pickles

1 gallon whole dill pickles

5 pounds sugar

Tabasco as needed

5 garlic cloves, chopped

- Drain pickles completely. Slice pickles.
- Return pickles to the original jar in five layers in the following order: pickles, sugar, Tabasco and garlic. Pack firmly into the original jar and close lid tightly.
- Let stand at room temperature for six days, turning the jar upside down once a day.
- After the sixth day, store in refrigerator.

Sweet and Sour Pickles

1 quart dill pickles, sliced, reserve juice

1½ cups sugar

½ cup white vinegar

¾ teaspoon mustard seeds

- Set aside juice and pickle jar. Place pickles in a bowl and cover with sugar. Let soak overnight.
- Place pickles back in jar.
- Heat juice, vinegar and mustard seeds to a boiling point and pour over pickles. Let set overnight.

Overnight Onions

1 pound purple onions, sliced

1 cup tarragon vinegar

½ cup sugar

½ teaspoon salt and pepper

• Place onion rings in a large jar.

• Pour in the vinegar, sugar, ½ teaspoon pepper, ½ teaspoon salt and 1 cup water.

• Cover tightly and shake well until the sugar is dissolved. Store in refrigerator overnight before serving.

Fun-to-Make Sweet Pickles

1 quart whole sour pickles

3¼ cups sugar

1 clove garlic, finely chopped

½ teaspoon ground cloves

• Pour off liquid from pickles; discard.

• Slice pickles in ¼-inch slices and place in large bowl. Add sugar, garlic and cloves. Mix and leave at room temperature until sugar is dissolved.

• Spoon all back into jar. Seal and refrigerate. Ready to eat after 3 days.

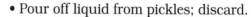

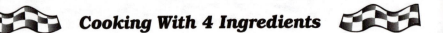

Cream Cheese Sandwiches

2 (8 ounce) packages
   cream cheese, softened
1 (4 ounce) can black
   olives, chopped
¾ cups finely chopped
   pecans
Pumpernickel rye bread

- Beat the cream cheese until creamy. Fold in olives and pecans.
- Trim crusts on bread.
- Spread cream cheese on bread.
- Slice sandwich into 3 finger strips.

Luncheon Sandwich

1 loaf thinly sliced,
   sandwich bread
2 sticks butter, softened
1 (5 ounce) jar cheese
   spread, softened
½ teaspoon
   worcestershire sauce

- Trim crust on the bread.
- With mixer, beat together the butter and cheese spread until smooth and creamy, adding worcestershire sauce.
- Spread mixture on three slices of bread making a triple decker sandwich.
- Place fourth slice of bread on top. Cut into finger sandwiches.

  These sandwiches can be served cold or warmed at 300° for 5 or 10 minutes.

Party Sandwiches

1 pound bacon, cooked,
   crumbled
½ cup ripe olives,
   coarsely chopped
½ cup chopped pecans
1¼ cups mayonnaise

- Mix all ingredients together.
- Spread on thin sliced white bread.
- Cut sandwiches into three strips.

Watercress Tea Sandwiches

1 small bunch of
watercress

5 hard boiled eggs, peeled

6 tablespoons
mayonnaise

1 tablespoon dijon
mustard

- Trim ½ of the watercress stems. Save the rest for garnish.

- In a food processor, coarsely chop the eggs; add mayonnaise, mustard and a little salt. Process until smooth.

- Fold in the chopped watercress and chill.

- Add mixture on thinly sliced white bread that has the crust trimmed. Cut into finger sandwiches.

Cream Cheese Tea Sandwiches

1 (8 ounce) package
cream cheese, softened

½ pound bacon, fried and
finely chopped

12-14 slices whole wheat
bread

1 (12 ounce) package
bean sprouts

- With a mixer, beat the cream cheese until smooth. Add the finely chopped bacon (or you can chop the cream cheese and bacon together in a food processor).

- On 6 to 8 slices of bread, spread the bacon-cream cheese mixture. Add a layer of bean sprouts.

- On the other 6 to 8 slices, spread either mayonnaise or butter and place on top of the bean sprouts making 6 or 8 sandwiches.

- With a sharp knife remove crust and cut each sandwich in 3 finger shapes. Refrigerate.

Cream Cheese Sandwich Spread

2 (8 ounce) packages
cream cheese, softened

1 (2½ ounce) jar dried
beef, finely chopped

1 bunch fresh green
onions and tops,
chopped

¾ cup mayonnaise, 1
teaspoon seasoned
pepper

- Combine all ingredients together until the mixture will spread smoothly.
- Trim crust of whole wheat bread and spread cream cheese mixture on bread.
- Top with another slice of bread and slice into 3 strips or 4 quarters.

Green Chili Grilled Cheese

4 slices bread

4 slices cheddar cheese

1 (4 ounce) can chopped
green chilies, drained

3 tablespoons margarine,
softened

- On 2 slices of bread, place a slice of cheese on each slice. Sprinkle with green chilies.
- Top with the two remaining slices of cheese; then with remaining two slices of bread.
- Butter the outside of the sandwiches.
- In a large skillet over medium heat brown sandwiches on both sides until golden brown and cheese has melted.

Confetti Sandwiches

1 tablespoon lemon juice

1 (8 ounce) package
cream cheese, softened

½ cup grated carrots

¼ cup each grated
cucumber, purple
onion and bell pepper

- Combine lemon juice with cream cheese; adding enough mayonnaise to make cheese into spreading consistency.
- Fold in grated vegetables and spread on bread for sandwiches. Refrigerate.

Hot Bunwiches

8 hamburger buns

8 slices Swiss cheese

8 slices ham, 8 slices turkey

8 slices American cheese

- Lay out all 8 buns. On the bottom bun, place the slices of Swiss cheese, ham, turkey and American cheese.
- Place the top bun over the American cheese.
- Wrap each bunwich individually in foil and place in freezer.
- When ready to serve, take out of freezer 2 to 3 hours before serving. Heat at 325° for about 30 minutes. Serve hot.

Reubens on a Bun

1 pound smoked frankfurters (8 per pound)

8 hot dog buns

1 (8 ounce) can sauerkraut, well drained

Caraway seeds

- Pierce each frankfurter and place into split buns.
- Arrange two tablespoons sauerkraut over each frank. Sprinkle with caraway seed.
- Place in a 9 x 13-inch shallow pan and drizzle with Thousand Island dressing.
- Heat just until hot dogs are thoroughly heated.

Italian Sausage Sandwiches

1 pound sweet Italian sausage, cooked, casing removed

1 red bell pepper, chopped

1 onion, chopped

1⅔ cups Italian-style spaghetti sauce

- In a skillet over medium heat, cook sausage, bell pepper and onion until sausage is brown and no longer pink.
- Stir in spaghetti sauce and heat until boiling. Simmer for 5 minutes stirring constantly.
- Pour mixture over split hoagie rolls.

Pizza Burger

1 pound lean ground beef

½ teaspoon salt

½ cup pizza sauce

4 slices mozzarella cheese

- Combine beef, salt and ½ pizza sauce.
- Mold into 4 patties and pan fry over medium heat for 5 to 6 minutes on each side.
- Just before burgers are done, top each with a spoonful of pizza sauce and a slice of cheese.
- Serve on a hamburger bun.

Marshmallow Sandwiches

1 jar marshmallow cream

Chunky peanut butter

White bread or whole wheat bread

Vanilla wafers, optional

- On one slice of bread, spread marshmallow cream.
- On a second slice of bread, spread the peanut butter.
- Put the marshmallow and the peanut butter sides together.

Ranch Cheeseburgers

1 packet ranch-style salad dressing mix

1 pound lean ground beef

1 cup shredded cheddar cheese

4 large hamburger buns, toasted

- Combine dressing mix with beef and cheese.
- Shape into four patties.
- Cook on charcoal grill until thoroughly cooked and browned.

Barking Dogs

10 wieners
5 slices cheese
10 corn tortillas
Oil

- Slice wieners lengthwise and halfway through.
- Cut each cheese slice in half and place inside each wiener.
- Wrap tortillas around wiener and secure with a toothpick.
- Heat several inches of oil in frying pan. Fry dogs in oil until tortilla is crisp. Serve hot.

Cheese Doggies

Sliced frankfurters
Cheddar cheese slices
Bacon slices
Hot dog buns

- Use 1 bacon slice for each frankfurter. Place bacon on paper towel or paper plate and cover with a paper towel and microwave for 45 seconds or until almost crisp.
- Cut lengthwise pocket in the frankfurter and stuff with a strip of cheese.
- Wrap bacon around the doggie and secure with toothpick.
- Place in split hot dog bun and microwave for about 30 seconds or until the hot dog is warm.

Dogs or Something

8 wieners
8 slices cheese
1 (8 ounce) package refrigerated crescent rolls

- Split wieners lengthwise and fill with a folded cheese slice.
- Wrap in a crescent dough roll and bake at 375° for about 12 minutes. Serve with mustard.

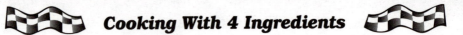

Hot and Sweet Mustard

4 ounces dry mustard

1 cup vinegar

3 eggs

1 cup sugar

• Soak dry mustard in vinegar overnight.

• Beat eggs and sugar together; then add to vinegar-mustard mixture.

• In top of double boiler, cook over low heat for about 15 minutes, stirring constantly. Mixture will resemble a custard consistency. Pour immediately into jars. Store in refrigerator. Serve with ham.

Great to keep in the refrigerator for ham sandwiches.

Avocado Butter

2 large avocados, peeled

2 tablespoons lime juice

1 pound butter, softened

¼ teaspoon ginger

• Combine all ingredients in electric blender or food processor. Blend until smooth.

• Serve on crackers or make party sandwiches on white or rye bread.

VEGETABLES
&
SIDE DISHES

Posh Squash

8 medium yellow squash, sliced

½ green bell pepper, seeded, chopped

1 small onion, chopped

1 (8 ounce) package Mexican Velveeta cheese, cubed

• Combine squash, bell pepper and onion in a large saucepan and just barely cover with water.

• Cook just until tender – about 10 to 15 minutes.

• Drain and add cheese; stir until cheese is melted and pour into a buttered 2-quart baking dish.

• Bake at 350° for 15 minutes.

Squash on the Run

5 medium yellow squash, sliced

2 thinly sliced potatoes

1 onion, chopped

2 cans cream of chicken soup

• In a buttered 2-quart casserole dish, layer the squash, potatoes and onion.

• In a saucepan, combine soup and ¾ can water; heat just enough to mix well. Pour over vegetables.

• Cover and bake at 350° for 45 minutes.

Seasoned Squash and Onion

8 yellow squash, sliced

2 onions, chopped

½ stick margarine

1 cup grated American cheese

• Cook squash and onion in a small amount of water until tender; drain.

• Add margarine and cheese and toss. Serve hot.

Dilled Zucchini

1 stick butter

8 medium zucchini, grated

1½ tablespoons dried dill weed

Salt and pepper

• In a skillet melt the butter and saute the zucchini and dill weed. Cook on medium heat for 5 minutes or just until tender.

Add salt and pepper and serve hot.

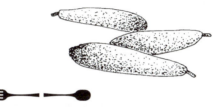

Stuffed Yellow Squash

5 large yellow squash

1 (16 ounce) package frozen chopped spinach

1 (8 ounce) package cream cheese

1 envelope dry onion soup mix

• Steam squash whole until tender.

• Slit squash lengthwise and remove the seeds with a spoon.

• Cook spinach according to package directions. Drain well. When spinach is cooked add the cream cheese which has been cut into small pieces and stir until it melts. Do not let this boil as the heat will be too hot for the cream cheese. Add soup mix, blending well.

• Fill scooped out squash shells with spinach mixture and top with a few sprinkles of cheddar cheese.

• Place on a baking sheet and bake at 325° for about 15 minutes.

Squash Casserole

6 medium yellow squash, sliced

1 yellow onion, chopped

1 (8 ounce) jar processed cheese spread

1 (4 ounce) can chopped green chilies

• Boil squash and onion until tender. Drain well and mix with cheese and chilies.

• Pour into buttered 7 x 11-inch baking dish. Bake 15 minutes at 375°.

Sunny Yellow Squash

6-8 medium yellow squash

1 (8 ounce) package cream cheese, softened

2 tablespoons margarine

1 teaspoon sugar

• In saucepan, cut up squash, add a little water and boil until tender. Drain.

• Add cream cheese that has been cubed, margarine, sugar and a little salt and pepper.

• Cook over low heat, stirring until cream cheese has melted.

Fried Zucchini

3 large zucchini, grated

5 eggs

1 pack Ritz crackers (⅓ of a 12 ounce box), crushed

½ cup grated parmesan cheese

• Combine the zucchini, eggs and cracker crumbs mixing well. Add cheese and a little salt and pepper.

• Drop by spoonfuls into a skillet with a little oil. Fry for about 15 minutes. Brown on each side.

Zucchini Patties

1½ cups grated zucchini
1 egg, beaten
2 tablespoons flour
⅓ cup finely minced onion

• Mix all ingredients together, adding ½ teaspoon seasoned salt.

• Heat a skillet with about 3 tablespoons oil.

• Drop zucchini mixture by tablespoons onto the skillet at medium high heat. Turn and brown both sides. Remove and drain on paper towels.

Cheesy Zucchini

5-6 medium zucchini, sliced in round
1 cup grated monterey jack cheese
⅔ cup breadcrumbs
1 (15 ounce) can Mexican stewed tomatoes

• Boil zucchini for 8 minutes until crisp-tender; drain.

• Place ½ of zucchini in greased 2-quart casserole and sprinkle with cheese and crumbs. Top with remainder of zucchini.

• Cover with stewed tomatoes.

• Bake 30 minutes at 350°.

Zucchini Beau Monde

6-8 medium zucchini, sliced
1 teaspoon beau monde seasoning
1 (8 ounce) carton sour cream
¼ cup grated parmesan cheese

• Saute zucchini in 2 tablespoons of margarine. Cook on low for about 5 minutes.

• Stir in seasoning, sour cream and cheese. Heat but do not boil.

Walnut Zucchini

6-8 zucchini, julienned

½ red bell pepper, julienned

½ stick margarine

1 cup chopped walnuts

• Saute zucchini and bell pepper in margarine until tender, shaking the pan and tossing the zucchini to cook evenly. Pour off any excess margarine.

• Add the chopped walnuts, some salt and pepper. When walnuts are well blended and heated, serve hot.

Mushrooms and Corn

4 ounces fresh mushrooms, sliced

3 chopped green onions and tops

2 tablespoons margarine

1 (15 ounce) package frozen whole kernel corn

• Place all ingredients in a 2-quart saucepan and cook on medium heat for 5 to 10 minutes. Add salt and pepper to taste.

Italian Corn

1 (16 ounce) package frozen whole kernel corn

2 slices bacon, cooked and diced

1 onion, chopped

1 (16 ounce) can Italian stewed tomatoes

• Place all ingredients in a 2-quart size pan.

• Cook until most of the liquid in the tomatoes has cooked out. Add a little salt and pepper. Serve hot.

Corn Casserole

2 (15 ounce) cans
    creamed corn

½ stick margarine, melted

1 cup seasoned
    breadcrumbs

1 bell pepper, chopped

• Mix all ingredients and pour into 2-quart casserole. Bake at 350° for 30 minutes.

Corn Au Gratin

3 cans mexicorn, drained

1 (4 ounce) can sliced
    mushrooms, drained

1 (10½ ounce) can cream
    of mushroom soup

1 cup shredded cheddar
    cheese

• Mix all ingredients together in a saucepan and heat slowly until cheese is melted. Serve hot.

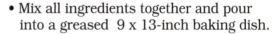

Super Corn Casserole

1 (15 ounce) can whole
    kernel corn

1 (15 ounce) can cream-
    style corn

1 stick margarine, melted

1 (8 ounce) carton sour
    cream

1 (6 ounce) package
    jalapeno cornbread mix

• Mix all ingredients together and pour into a greased 9 x 13-inch baking dish.

• Bake uncovered at 350° for 35 minutes.

Corn Ole

2 (16 ounce) cans whole kernel corn, drained

1 (8 ounce) package cream cheese

1 (4 ounce) can chopped green chilies

1 (2 ounce) jar pimento

• Combine ingredients in saucepan.

• Simmer over low heat until cheese melts, mixing well.

Calico Corn

1 (16 ounce) package frozen whole kernel corn

1 bell pepper, chopped

⅓ cup chopped celery

1 (10½ ounce) can cream of cheddar cheese soup

• Cook corn in microwave according to package directions; drain well.

• To the corn add the bell pepper and celery. Stir in soup; mixing well.

• Pour into a buttered 2-quart casserole and bake covered at 350° for 30 minutes.

Corn Pudding

1 (8 ounce) package corn muffin mix

1 (15 ounce) can cream-style corn

½ cup sour cream

3 eggs, slightly beaten

• Combine all ingredients and pour into a buttered 2-quart baking dish.

• Bake uncovered at 350° for about 35 minutes.

Corn Maize

½ stick margarine, melted

1 (3 ounce) package cream cheese, softened

2 (15 ounce) cans whole kernel corn, drained

⅓ cup salsa

• Mix margarine and cream cheese together. Add corn and salsa sauce.

• Pour into a 2-quart buttered baking dish.

• Bake covered at 350° for about 25 minutes. Serve hot.

Shoepeg Corn

1 (8 ounce) package cream cheese, softened

1 stick butter, softened

3 (15 ounce) cans shoepeg corn

1 (4 ounce) can chopped green chilies

• With mixer or fork, combine the butter and cream cheese. Add corn and green chilies, mixing well.

• Spoon into a 7 x 11-inch greased casserole.

• Bake covered at 350° for 30 minutes.

Corn Bake

2 (15 ounce) cans creamed corn

1 (8 ounce) package corn muffin mix

2 eggs, beaten

1 stick margarine, melted

• Mix all ingredients and pour into a greased 9 x 13-inch baking dish.

• Bake at 350° for 45 minutes.

Baked Beans and Corn

1 (15 ounce) can ranch-style beans

1 (15 ounce) can pork and beans

1 (15 ounce) whole kernel corn, drained

1 (15 ounce) can chili without beans

• Combine all ingredients. Spoon into a lightly greased 3-quart baking dish.

• Bake at 300° for one hour.

Classic Baked Beans

⅓ cup packed brown sugar

1 tablespoon mustard

⅓ cup ketchup

2 (15 ounce) cans pork and beans

• Combine all ingredients.

• Bake at 325° for 1 hour.

Chili Baked Beans

2 (16 ounce) cans pork and beans

1 (15 ounce) can chili with beans

¼ cup molasses

1 teaspoon chili powder

• Pour visible liquid out of can of pork and beans.

• In a 2-quart casserole combine pork and beans, chili, molasses and chili powder. Heat until bubbly.

Italian Broiled Tomatoes

4 medium tomatoes

Salt and pepper

½ teaspoon dried oregano

Italian salad dressing

- Core tomatoes and cut in half crosswise.
- Make a shallow crisscross cut on the surface of the tomatoes. Season the cut surface with salt, pepper and oregano; drizzle with salad dressing.
- Broil, cut side up for about 5 minutes or until heated thoroughly.

Tomato Casserole

2 (15 ounce) cans Mexican-style stewed tomatoes

2 onions, sliced

1¼ cups cracker crumbs

1 cup shredded cheddar cheese

- In a 2-quart casserole layer the tomatoes, onions, cracker crumbs and cheese; repeat layers.
- Sprinkle a little salt and pepper. Bake at 350° for 45 minutes.

Tasty Turnips

6 medium turnips

2 teaspoons sugar

1 teaspoon salt

½ stick butter (not margarine), melted

- Peel and dice turnips. Boil with sugar and salt until tender. Drain.
- Add butter to turnips and mash. Serve hot.

Lima Beans

1 (16 ounce) package
  frozen baby lima beans
1 cup chopped celery
3 tablespoons margarine
2 teaspoons lemon juice

- Place lima beans, celery, margarine and lemon juice in a 2-quart saucepan and add ⅓ cup water.
- Cook until vegetables are tender crisp. You may add salt and pepper if you like.

Snow Peas and Mushrooms

1 cup fresh sliced
  mushrooms
3 tablespoons margarine
1 (10 ounce) package
  frozen snow peas
1 tablespoon soy sauce

- Saute mushrooms in margarine. Stir in snow peas and soy sauce.
- Cook the length of time on package directions. Toss and serve.

Tasty Black-Eyed Peas

2 (10 ounce) packages
  frozen black-eyed peas
1¼ cups chopped green
  pepper
¾ cup chopped onion
1 (15 ounce) can Mexican
  stewed tomatoes,
  undrained

- Cook black-eyes peas according to package directions; drain.
- Saute green pepper and onion in 3 tablespoons margarine. Add peas, tomatoes and a little salt and pepper; cook over low heat until thoroughly heated, stirring often.

Sauteed Celery

1 bunch celery, chopped diagonally

1 (8 ounce) can water chestnuts, drained and chopped

¼ cup almonds, toasted

½ stick margarine, melted

- Boil celery in salted water just until tender crisp. Drain.
- Saute the water chestnuts and almonds in the melted margarine.
- Toss together the celery and the water chestnuts-almond mixture. Serve hot.

Okra Gumbo

2 slices bacon, chopped

½ onion, chopped

1 (10 ounce) package frozen okra, sliced

1 (15 ounce) can stewed tomatoes, chopped

- Saute bacon, add onion and brown. Do not drain.
- Add frozen okra and stewed tomatoes.
- Cook over low heat until okra is tender.

Fried Okra

Fresh garden okra, small size

Milk or buttermilk

Corn meal

Salt and pepper

- Thoroughly wash and drain okra. Cut off top and ends and slice.
- Toss okra with a little milk or buttermilk (just enough to make the cornmeal stick). Sprinkle cornmeal over okra and toss.
- Heat 2 or 3 tablespoons of oil in skillet. Fry okra, turning several times until okra is golden brown and crisp.

Honey Carrots

¼ cup honey

½ stick margarine, melted

⅓ cup packed brown sugar

2 (15 ounce) cans carrots, drained

• Combine honey, margarine and brown sugar. Stir well and pour over carrots.

• Cook over low heat until heated thoroughly.

Tangy Carrot Coins

2 (15 ounce) cans sliced carrots

¼ stick margarine

2 tablespoons brown sugar

1 tablespoon dijon mustard

• Place all ingredients in a saucepan. Cook and stir over medium heat for about 2 minutes. Serve hot.

Sweet Carrots

2 (16 ounce) cans sliced carrots

⅓ cup peach preserves

2 tablespoons margarine, melted

¼ teaspoon salt

• Combine carrots with peach preserves and margarine. Add salt.

• Cook over low heat until carrots are heated thoroughly.

Dilled Carrots

1 (12 ounce) package
   fresh baby carrots
3 chicken bouillon cubes
   or 2 teaspoons bouillon
   granules
¾ stick butter
2 teaspoons dill weed

- Boil carrots in water with dissolved bouillon cubes until tender (about 8 minutes). Drain.
- Place in a skillet with melted butter. Cook on low heat for only a few minutes making sure the butter coats all carrots.
- Sprinkle dill weed over carrots and shake to make sure dill is on all carrots. Place in serving dish and serve immediately.

Glazed Carrots

1 (16 ounce) package
   frozen baby carrots
¼ cup apple cider
¼ cup apple jelly
1½ teaspoons dijon
   mustard

- In saucepan place carrots and apple cider and bring to boil. Reduce heat. Cover and simmer about 8 minutes until carrots are tender.
- Remove cover and cook on medium heat until liquid evaporates; stir in jelly and mustard. Cook until jelly melts and the carrots are glazed.

Brown Sugar Carrots

2 (15 ounce) cans carrots
½ stick margarine
3 tablespoons brown
   sugar
½ teaspoon ground ginger

- Drain carrots but reserve 2 tablespoons liquid.
- Combine the 2 tablespoons liquid with the margarine, brown sugar and ginger. Heat thoroughly.
- Add carrots, stirring gently and cook 3 minutes. Serve hot.

Speedy Cabbage

1 head cabbage, shredded
¼ stick margarine
3 tablespoons sour cream
½ teaspoon black pepper

• Saute cabbage in margarine and about 2 tablespoons water until tender (about 3 to 4 minutes) stirring constantly.

• Stir in sour cream and about ½ teaspoon salt, ½ teaspoon sugar and pepper. Serve hot.

Creamed Cabbage

1 head cabbage, shredded
1 (10½ ounce) can cream of celery soup
⅔ cup milk
1 (8 ounce) package shredded cheddar cheese

• Place cabbage in a 2-quart buttered baking dish.

• Pour celery soup diluted with milk over top of cabbage. Bake covered at 325° for 30 minutes.

• Remove from oven, sprinkle with cheese and bake uncovered another 5 minutes.

Fried Cabbage

1 small head cabbage, finely chopped
½ teaspoon salt
3 tablespoons oil
2 tablespoons Italian salad dressing

• Sprinkle cabbage with salt and set aside for 30 minutes.

• Heat oil in skillet until very hot. Add the cabbage and stir fry about 5 minutes.

• Remove and add Italian dressing.

Cheesy Baked Eggplant

1 eggplant

½ cup mayonnaise

⅔ cup seasoned breadcrumbs

¼ cup grated parmesan cheese

- Peel eggplant and slice ½-inch thick.
- Spread both sides with mayonnaise and dip in mixture of crumbs and cheese. Coat both sides well.
- Place in a single layer in a shallow baking dish. Bake at 400° for 20 minutes.

Eggplant Casserole

1 large eggplant

1 cup cracker crumbs

1 cup shredded cheddar cheese, divided

1 (10 ounce) can tomatoes and green chilies

- Peel and slice eggplant.
- Place in a saucepan and cover with water. Cook 10 minutes or until tender. Drain well on paper towels.
- Mash eggplant. Stir in crackers, ¾ cup of the cheese and tomatoes; mix well.
- Spoon eggplant in a 1-quart buttered baking dish. Sprinkle with remaining cheese. Bake at 350° for about 30 minutes.

Spicy Hominy

1 (15 ounce) can yellow hominy, drained

1 (8 ounce) carton sour cream

1 (4 ounce) can chopped green chilies

1¼ cups grated cheddar cheese

- Combine all ingredients, adding a little salt. Pour into a one-quart baking dish and bake at 350° for about 20 minutes.

Baked Eggplant

1 medium eggplant

½ stick butter, melted

1 (5 ounce) can
  evaporated milk

1½ cups cracker crumbs

- Peel, slice and boil eggplant until easily mashed; drain. Season with a little salt and pepper.
- Add all other ingredients.
- Pour into a 2-quart buttered baking dish. Bake at 350° for 25 minutes.

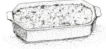

Hominy

1 (8 ounce) jar of jalapeno
  processed cheese
  spread

2 (15 ounce) cans of
  golden yellow hominy

1 (8 ounce) carton sour
  cream

1 teaspoon seasoned salt

- Heat processed cheese spread in microwave (lid off) just enough for cheese to mix with hominy. Combine hominy, sour cream and processed cheese spread.
- Pour into a 2-quart casserole dish and bake at 350° for about 30 minutes or until bubbly and lightly brown on top.

Baked Onions

4 large onions, thinly
  sliced

1½ cups crushed potato
  chips

1 cup shredded cheddar
  cheese

1 (10½ ounce) can cream
  of chicken soup

- In a 9 x 13-inch baking dish alternate layers of onion, potato chips and cheese.
- Spoon soup over the last layer and pour ¼ cup milk or ¼ cup water on top. Sprinkle with a little red or black pepper.
- Bake at 300° for 1 hour.

Cheesy Baked Onions

4 yellow onions, peeled, sliced

1 stick margarine

25 Ritz crackers, crushed

⅓ cup grated parmesan cheese

- Saute onions in margarine until transparent.
- Spread ½ of the onions in a 2-quart buttered casserole dish. Top with ½ of the crackers, ½ of the cheese. Repeat layers.
- Bake uncovered at 325° for 30 minutes.

Onion Casserole

5-6 medium mild onions, thinly sliced

3 tablespoons margarine

1 cup milk

4 eggs

- Saute onions in margarine in covered skillet for about 30 minutes. Cool.
- In bowl beat together milk and eggs. Stir in onions and transfer to greased baking dish. Bake at 325° for 45 to 50 minutes or until light golden.

Easy Onions

6 medium white onions, peeled and cored

6 beef bouillon cubes

Worcestershire

½ stick margarine, melted

- Place each onion in a piece of heavy-duty aluminum foil.
- Place a bouillon cube in each onion cavity and several drops of worcestershire. Fill cavity up with margarine and wrap tightly in foil. Place on grill and cook 40 to 45 minutes. (Onion can be baked in the oven at 350° for 30 to 40 minutes.)

Cheesy Onion Casserole

5 sweet onions, sliced

1 stick margarine

1 cup shredded cheddar cheese

22 saltine crackers, crushed

- Saute onion in margarine until soft.
- In a buttered 2-quart casserole layer half the onions, half the cheese, half the crackers. Repeat layers.
- Bake at 325° for 35 minutes.

Spinach To Like

2 (10 ounce) packages frozen, chopped spinach

1 (8 ounce) carton sour cream

½ package dry onion soup mix

⅔ cup seasoned breadcrumbs

- Cook spinach according to package directions; drain well. Add sour cream and onion soup mix to the spinach.
- Pour into a 2-quart casserole. Sprinkle breadcrumbs on top. Bake at 350° for 35 minutes.

Spinach Onion Casserole

2 (16 ounce) packages frozen chopped spinach

1 (10 ½ ounce) can cream of chicken soup

1 envelope dry onion soup mix

¾ cup cracker crumbs

- Thaw spinach, press out water. Mix with sour cream and dry onion soup mix.
- Pour into a 2-quart baking dish. Sprinkle with cracker crumbs.
- Bake at 325° for 20 to 25 minutes.

Cheezy Spinach Bake

1 (16 ounce) carton
cottage cheese

1 (8 ounce) package
grated cheddar cheese

1 (10 ounce) package
chopped spinach, well
drained

3 eggs, beaten

• Combine all ingredients and mix well.

• Spoon into a buttered 7 x 11-inch
baking dish.

• Bake at 350° for 45 minutes.

Creamed Spinach Bake

1 (16 ounce) package
frozen chopped spinach

2 (3 ounce) packages
cream cheese, softened

3 tablespoons margarine

1 cup Italian-style
seasoned breadcrumbs

• In a saucepan, cook spinach, with ¾
cup water for 6 minutes; drain. Add
cream cheese and margarine to the
spinach; heat until cream cheese and
margarine are melted and mixed well
with the spinach.

• Pour into a greased 2-quart baking dish.
Sprinkle a little salt over spinach; then
cover with the breadcrumbs.

• Bake uncovered at 350° for 15 to 20
minutes.

Baked Onion Rings

2 egg whites, slightly
beaten

Salt and pepper to taste

1 large sweet yellow
onion, cut into rings

¾ cup dry breadcrumbs

• Mix egg whites, salt and pepper.

• Dip onion rings into egg whites and then
coat with breadcrumbs. Place in single
layer on greased baking sheet.

• Bake at 425° for 10 to 15 minutes.

Herbed Spinach

2 (16 ounce) packages
  frozen chopped spinach

1 (8 ounce) package
  cream cheese, softened

½ stick margarine, melted

1 (6 ounce) package
  herbed stuffing

• Cook spinach as directed on package. Drain and add the cream cheese and ½ of the margarine. Season with a little salt and pepper.

• Pour into a buttered casserole dish. Spread the herb stuffing on top and then drizzle with the remaining margarine.

• Bake at 350° for 25 minutes.

Favorite Spinach

2 (10 ounce) packages
  frozen chopped
  spinach, thawed, well
  drained

1 package dry onion soup
  mix

1 (8 ounce) carton sour
  cream

⅔ cup shredded monterey
  jack cheese

• Combine the spinach, onion soup mix and sour cream. Pour into a buttered 2-quart baking dish. Bake at 350° for 20 minutes.

• Take out of oven and sprinkle cheese over the top and place casserole back in oven for 5 minutes.

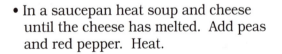

Cheezy Peas Please

1 (10½ ounce) can cream
  of mushroom soup

1 (6 ounce) roll garlic
  cheese

2 (15 ounce) cans green
  peas, drained

⅛ teaspoon red pepper

• In a saucepan heat soup and cheese until the cheese has melted. Add peas and red pepper. Heat.

Spinach Bake

2 (8 ounce) packages
  cream cheese, softened

1 (10½ ounce) can cream
  of chicken soup,
  undiluted

2 (16 ounce) packages
  frozen chopped
  spinach, thawed, well
  drained

1 cup crushed Ritz
  crackers

• In mixing bowl, beat the cream cheese
  until smooth. Add soup; mix well.

• Stir in spinach. Spoon into a well
  greased 3-quart baking dish.

• Sprinkle cracker crumbs over top of
  casserole. Bake uncovered at 325° for
  35 minutes.

Creamed Peas and Potatoes

2 pounds small new
  potatoes, quartered

1 (10½ ounce) can cream
  of mushroom soup

⅓ cup milk

1 (10 ounce) package
  frozen peas with pearl
  onions

• Cook new potatoes about 25 minutes or
  until tender.

• Add soup, milk, ½ teaspoon black
  pepper and the peas, stirring occasionally.

Seasoned Green Beans

4 slices bacon, chopped

1 medium onion, chopped

2 (15 ounce) cans green
  beans, drained

1 teaspoon sugar

• Saute bacon and onion in skillet. Drain.

• Add green beans and sugar and heat
  thoroughly.

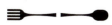

Italian Green Beans

1 (16 ounce) package
  frozen Italian green
  beans

3 green onions and tops,
  chopped

2 tablespoons margarine

1 teaspoon mixed Italian
  seasoning

• Mix all ingredients in a 2-quart saucepan and cook according to package
  directions.

Green Beans

1 pound fresh green
  beans

2 tablespoons soy sauce

¼ teaspoon ground
  nutmeg

½ cup toasted sesame
  seeds

• Cook green beans until tender crisp,
  about 10 minutes.

• Combine the soy sauce, nutmeg and 2
  tablespoons margarine. Cook over
  medium heat for a few minutes.

• Add to green beans and toss lightly.

• Add sesame seeds, toss again.

Crunchy Green Beans

3 (15 ounce) cans whole
  green beans

2 cans cream of
  mushroom soup

2 (11 ounce) cans water
  chestnuts, chopped

2 cans french fried onion
  rings

• Combine green beans, mushroom soup,
  water chestnuts, ½ teaspoon of salt and
  a little pepper.

• Pour into a 2-quart casserole. Bake
  covered at 350° for 30 minutes.

• Remove casserole from oven and
  sprinkle onion rings over top and bake
  10 minutes longer.

Green Beans and Almonds

2 (16 ounce) packages frozen french cut green beans

¼ stick margarine

2 (8 ounce) cans water chestnuts, chopped

½ cup slivered almonds, toasted

- Cook beans according to the package directions.
- Drain, add margarine and heat just until margarine melts. Fold in water chestnuts.
- Place in serving dish and sprinkle almonds over the top.

Souper Cauliflower

1 (16 ounce) package frozen cauliflower, cooked, drained

1 (10½ ounce) can cream of celery soup

¼ cup milk

1 cup shredded cheddar cheese

- Place cauliflower in a 2-quart greased baking dish.
- In a saucepan, combine soup, milk and cheese; heat just enough to mix well. Pour over cauliflower.
- Bake at 350° for 15 minutes.

Savory Cauliflower

1 head cauliflower

1 (1.25 ounce) envelope hollandaise sauce mix

Fresh parsley to garnish

Lemon slices to garnish, optional

- Cut cauliflower into small flowerets. Cook in salted water until barely tender. Do not overcook.
- Mix sauce as directed on package.
- Drain cauliflower, top with sauce and a sprinkling of parsley.

Cauliflower Whiz

1 head cauliflower

1 jar jalapeno processed cheese spread, melted

- Place cauliflower on a microwaveable plate. Cover with plastic wrap leaving a 1-inch vent opening. For each pound of cauliflower, microwave on high for 7 minutes.

- When done remove plastic wrap and pour melted processed cheese spread over top.

Best Cauliflower

1 (16 ounce) package frozen cauliflower

1 (8 ounce) carton sour cream

1½ cups grated American or cheddar cheese

4 teaspoons sesame seeds, toasted

- Cook cauliflower as directed on package.

- Drain and place half of cauliflower in a 2-quart baking dish. Sprinkle a little salt and pepper on cauliflower. Spread one half of the sour cream and one half of the cheese. Top with 2 teaspoons sesame seed. Repeat layers.

- Bake at 350° for about 15 to 20 minutes.

Shrimp and Almond Sauce for Broccoli

1 (10½ ounce) can cream of shrimp soup

1 (3 ounce) package cream cheese

1 tablespoon lemon juice

⅓ cup slivered almonds, toasted

- Cook a 16-ounce package of broccoli flowerets.

- Combine in saucepan the shrimp soup, cream cheese and lemon juice. Heat slowly until cream cheese is melted.

- When ready to serve pour over cooked broccoli and sprinkle almonds over top of sauce.

Lemon Broccoli

2 (16 ounce) packages
broccoli flowerets

½ stick butter

1 tablespoon lemon juice

½ teaspoon seasoning
salt

- Cook broccoli according to package directions; drain.
- Melt butter and stir in lemon juice and seasoned salt.
- Pour over broccoli and toss to coat.

Tomatoes and Broccoli

1 (10 ounce) package
frozen chopped
broccoli

1½ cups grated monterey
jack cheese, divided

¼ cup finely chopped
onion

3 large tomatoes, halved
horizontally

- Cook broccoli as directed on package. Drain and mix with 1 cup of cheese. Add onion.
- Place tomato halves in greased baking dish. Place broccoli mixture on each tomato half and top with remaining cheese.
- Broil at 350° for 10 to 12 minutes.

Cheddar Broccoli Bake

1 (10½ ounce) can
cheddar cheese soup

½ cup milk

1 (16 ounce) bag frozen
broccoli flowerets,
cooked

1 can french-fried onion
rings

- In 2-quart casserole, mix soup, milk, and broccoli.
- Bake at 350° for 25 minutes.
- Stir. Sprinkle onions over broccoli mixture.
- Bake 5 more minutes or until onions are golden.

Broccoli Stuffed Tomatoes

4 medium tomatoes

1 (10 ounce) package frozen chopped broccoli

1 (6 ounce) roll garlic cheese, softened

½ teaspoon garlic salt

- Cut tops off tomatoes and scoop out pulp.
- Cook broccoli according to package instruction; drain well.
- Combine broccoli, cheese and garlic salt. Heat just until cheese is melted. Stuff broccoli mixture into tomatoes and place on baking sheet.
- Bake at 375° for about 10 minutes.

Asparagus Caesar

3 (15 ounce) cans asparagus spears, drained

½ stick margarine, melted

3 tablespoons lemon juice

½ cup grated parmesan cheese

- Place asparagus in a 2-quart baking dish. Drizzle on margarine and lemon juice. Sprinkle with cheese (and a little paprika if you like).
- Bake at 400° for 15 to 20 minutes.

Almond Asparagus

⅓ cup margarine

1 to 1½ pounds fresh asparagus

⅔ cup slivered almonds

1 tablespoon lemon juice

- Melt margarine in skillet, add the asparagus and almonds. Saute 3 to 4 minutes.
- Cover and steam about 2 minutes or until tender crisp.
- Sprinkle lemon and a little salt and pepper over asparagus. Serve hot.

Sesame Asparagus

6 fresh asparagus spears, trimmed

1 tablespoon margarine or butter

1 teaspoon lemon juice

1 teaspoon sesame seeds

- Place asparagus in a skillet. Sprinkle with salt if desired. Add ¼ cup water; bring to a boil. Reduce heat. Cover and simmer about 4 minutes.
- Melt the butter and add lemon juice and sesame seed.
- Drain asparagus; drizzled with the butter mixture.

Asparagus Ham Roll-Up

4 slices Swiss cheese

4 slices ham

2 (10½ ounce) cans asparagus spears

1 (10½ ounce) can cream of celery soup

- Place a slice of cheese on top of each ham slice.
- Put 3 asparagus spears on each ham-cheese slice. Roll up, secure with toothpick.
- Place in casserole, seam side down.
- In saucepan dilute soup with ⅓ cup water; heat just until well mixed. Pour over ham-cheese slices.
- Bake at 350° for 15 to 20 minutes.

Vegetable Medley

1 (16 ounce) package frozen broccoli, cauliflower and carrots

1 (16 ounce) package frozen corn

2 (10½ ounce) cans fiesta nacho cheese soup

½ cup milk

- Combine broccoli mixture and corn in a 2-quart greased baking dish.
- Combine fiesta nacho cheese soup and milk in a saucepan, heat just enough to mix well.
- Pour over vegetables.
- Cover and bake at 350° for about 30 minutes.

Roasted Vegetables

1½ pounds assorted fresh vegetables such as squash, carrots, red bell peppers, zucchini, cauliflower or broccoli

1 (11 ounce) can water chestnuts, drained

1 envelope savory herb with garlic soup mix

¼ stick margarine, melted

- Cut all vegetables in uniform 2-inch pieces and place in a greased 2-quart casserole dish with water chestnuts.

- Combine melted margarine and soup mix and drizzle over vegetables, stirring well.

- Cover and bake vegetables at 400° for 20 to 25 minutes or until tender, stirring once.

Buttered Vegetables

1 stick butter

2 yellow squash, sliced

1 (16 ounce) package broccoli flowerets

1 (10 ounce) box frozen corn

- Melt butter in large skillet and add all vegetables.

- Saute vegetables for about 10 to 15 minutes or until tender-crisp. Add a little salt if you like. Serve warm.

Herb Seasoned Vegetables

1 (14 ounce) can seasoned chicken broth with Italian herbs

½ teaspoon garlic powder

1 (16 ounce) package frozen vegetables (broccoli, cauliflower, etc.)

½ cup grated parmesan cheese

- Heat broth, garlic and vegetables to a boil. Cover and cook over low heat for 5 minutes or until tender-crisp. Drain.

- Place in serving dish and sprinkle cheese over vegetables.

Creamy Vegetable Casserole

1 (16 ounce) package
frozen broccoli, carrots
and cauliflower

1 (10½ ounce) can cream
of mushroom soup,
undiluted

1 (8 ounce) carton
spreadable garden
vegetable cream cheese

1 cup seasoned croutons

- Cook vegetables according to package directions; drain and place in a large bowl.
- In a saucepan, place the soup and cream cheese; heat just enough to mix easily.
- Pour into the vegetable mixture, mixing well.
- Pour into a 2-quart baking dish. Sprinkle with croutons. Bake uncovered at 375° for 25 minutes or until bubbly.

Veggies To Love

1 (16 ounce) package
frozen broccoli,
cauliflower and carrot
combination

1 can cream of celery
soup

⅓ cup milk

1 (2.8 ounce) can french-
fried onions

- Cook vegetables according to package directions. Add soup and milk, mixing well.
- Pour into a buttered 2-quart baking dish and sprinkle french-fried onions over top.
- Bake at 350° for about 30 minutes or until bubbly.

Potatoes Supreme

1 (32 ounce) package
   frozen hash browned
   potatoes, thawed
1 onion, chopped
2 (10½ ounce) cans cream
   of chicken soup
1 (8 ounce) carton sour
   cream

- In a large bowl, combine potatoes, onion, soup and sour cream. Pour into a greased 9 x 13-inch baking dish.
- Bake covered at 350° for 1 hour.

This recipe is also good with ½ cup parmesan or cheddar cheese sprinkled on top about the last 5 minutes of baking.

Potatoes with a Zip

1 (32 ounce) bag frozen
   hash brown potatoes
1 (16 ounce) box Velveeta
   cheese, cubed
2 cups mayonnaise
1 (7 ounce) can chopped
   green chilies

- In a large bowl, combine hash browns, cheese, mayonnaise and green chilies.
- Spoon into a buttered 9 x 13-inch baking dish. Cover and bake at 325° for 1 hour.
- Stir twice during baking to prevent burning.

Creamy Cheesy Potatoes

1 (32 ounce) bag frozen
   hash brown potatoes
1 (16 ounce) box Velveeta
   cheese, cubed
1 (10½ ounce) can cream
   of chicken soup
1 (8 ounce) carton sour
   cream

- In a large bowl, combine hash browns, cheese, soup and sour cream. (You may want to add ½ teaspoon salt.)
- Spoon into a buttered 9 x 13-inch baking dish. Cover and bake at 325° for 1 hour.
- Stir twice during baking to prevent burning.

Twice Baked Potatoes

4 baked potatoes
½ stick margarine
¼ cup milk
1 cup grated cheddar
  cheese

- Bake potatoes. Cut cooked potatoes in half.
- Scoop out meat of the potato and whip with margarine and milk; add a little salt. Mound back into the potato halves.
- Sprinkle with grated cheese. Bake at 350° for 30 minutes.

Baked Potato Toppers

1 cup grated cheddar
  cheese
½ cup sour cream
¼ cup soft margarine,
  softened
4 tablespoons chopped
  green onion

- Mix all ingredients and serve on baked potato.

Golden Potato Casserole

1 (2 pound) bag frozen
  hash brown potatoes,
  thawed

1 pint sour cream

1 (8 ounce) bag shredded
  cheddar cheese

1 bunch chopped fresh
  green onions and tops,
  chopped

- Combine potatoes, sour cream, cheese and onion in a large bowl and thoroughly mix.
- Pour into a 9 x 13-inch buttered casserole dish. Sprinkle a little paprika on top.
- Cover and bake at 325° for 55 minutes.

Loaded Baked Potatoes

6 medium to large potatoes

1 (1 pound) hot sausage

1 (1 pound) box Velveeta cheese

1 (10 ounce) can tomatoes and green chilies

- Wrap potatoes in foil and bake at 375° for 1 hour or until done.
- Brown sausage and drain.
- Cut cheese into chunks and add to sausage.
- Heat until cheese is melted; add the tomatoes and green chilies.   Serve the sausage-cheese mixture over baked potatoes.

Vegetable Stuffed Potatoes

2 (10 ounce) cans fiesta nacho cheese soup

1 (16 ounce) bag frozen assorted vegetables, cooked, drained

8 large potatoes, baked

Black pepper

- In saucepan, heat nacho cheese and vegetables.
- Cut a lengthwise slice in the top of each potato.
- Slightly mash the pulp in each potato.
- Spoon sauce mixture onto each potato. Sprinkle with black pepper.

Broccoli Potatoes

5 baking potatoes

Margarine

1 (9 ounce) package frozen broccoli and cheese sauce

Paprika to garnish, optional

- Put the potatoes in a 400° oven for 1 hour. (Potatoes are thoroughly cooked when you can stick a fork in the center and potato is soft.)
- Just before serving, slit each potato lengthwise.
- Fluff potato up with a fork, adding margarine.
- Heat broccoli and cheese sauce in saucepan and pour over each potato.

Oven-Roasted Potatoes

2 pounds potatoes, unpeeled

1 envelope dry onion soup mix

⅓ cup oil

½ teaspoon black pepper

- Wash potatoes and cut into medium-size chunks.
- In a large plastic bag, add all ingredients. Shake until potatoes are evenly coated.
- Empty coated potatoes into a greased 9 x 13-inch baking pan.
- Bake uncovered at 425°, stirring twice, 40 minutes or until golden brown. Serves 8.

Philly Potatoes

4½ cups instant mashed potatoes, prepared, hot

2 tablespoons freeze-dried chives

1 (8 ounce) package cream cheese, softened

1 egg slightly beaten

- Mix all ingredients, blending well.
- Place in a greased 3-quart casserole.
- Bake covered at 350° for 30 minutes.
- Uncover and bake for 15 minutes more.

Company Potatoes

5 potatoes, peeled and sliced

2 (8 ounce) cartons whipping cream

2 tablespoons dijon mustard

⅓ cup grated parmesan cheese

- In a greased 9 x 13-inch baking dish, layer potatoes and add a little salt and pepper.
- In a saucepan, combine the cream, mustard, 2 tablespoons margarine and a little garlic powder; heat to boiling. Pour over potatoes.
- Cover and bake at 350° for 1 hour.
- Uncover and top with parmesan cheese. Bake 10 minutes longer or until potatoes are tender.

Cheddar Potatoes

1 (10½ ounce) can
cheddar cheese soup

⅓ cup sour cream

2 fresh green onions,
chopped

3 cups instant seasoned
mashed potatoes,
prepared

- In a saucepan, heat soup; add sour cream, onion and little black pepper.
- Stir in potatoes until well blended.
- Pour into a buttered 2-quart casserole.
- Cook at 350° for about 25 minutes.

Ranch Mashed Potatoes

4 cups instant, unsalted
mashed potatoes,
prepared

1 packet ranch-style
dressing mix

½ stick margarine

½ cup sour cream

- Combine all ingredients in saucepan.
- Heat on low until potatoes are thoroughly heated.

Potato Puff

3 eggs, separated

2 cups instant mashed
potatoes, prepared, hot

½ cup sour cream

2 teaspoons dried parsley

- Beat egg whites until stiff but still moist. Set aside.
- Beat yolks until smooth and add to potato mixture.
- Fold in the beaten egg whites, sour cream, parsley, 1 teaspoon seasoned salt and ½ teaspoon white pepper.
- Pour into a buttered 2-quart casserole. Bake uncovered at 350° for 45 minutes.

Cheesy Potatoes

10-12 new potatoes

1 (8 ounce) carton sour cream

½ stick margarine, melted

1 (1 pound) box Velveeta cheese, sliced

- Rinse and scrub potatoes well but do not peel. Cut into ¼-inch slices and place in a large saucepan; cover with water. Cook about 25 minutes until slightly tender. Drain.
- Place ½ of potatoes in a 9 x 13-inch baking dish. Sprinkle with salt and pepper.
- Spread half of sour cream and half of the melted margarine over top of potatoes. Put half the sliced cheese on top.
- Repeat layer. Bake at 400° about 20 minutes or until bubbly.

Baked New Potatoes

1 pound new potatoes, unpeeled

1 clove garlic, minced

1 large onion coarsely chopped

1 stick butter or margarine

- Par-boil new potatoes. Drain and quarter.
- In large skillet, saute onion and garlic with butter until onions start to become translucent. Add potatoes. Toss to coat.
- Place in large casserole dish. Add 1 teaspoon seasoned salt.
- Bake at 350°, basting occasionally, for 25 to 30 minutes until potatoes are fork tender.

Grilled New Potatoes

1 pound new potatoes

3 tablespoons orange
   marmalade

1 teaspoon brown sugar

2 tablespoons melted
   butter or margarine

- Cook new potatoes covered in boiling water until crisp-tender.
- Drain and cut in half. Thread on skewers.
- Combine next 3 ingredients and brush mixture over potatoes.
- Grill over medium hot coals until potatoes are browned, about 5 minutes each side. Salt and pepper to taste. Baste frequently. Can be baked at 400° for 20 minutes.

Mashed Red Potatoes

3 pounds red potatoes,
   quartered, unpeeled

⅓ cup whole milk

⅔ stick margarine

¼ teaspoon white pepper

- Place potatoes in a large saucepan and cover with water; adding 1 teaspoon salt. Cover and bring to a boil.
- Reduce heat; cook for 25 minutes or until very tender.
- Drain potatoes well and place in a large mixing bowl. Add the milk, butter, pepper and a little salt.
- Beat until potatoes are light and fluffy.

Potato Souffle

2⅔ cups instant mashed
   potatoes

2 eggs, beaten

1 cup shredded cheddar
   cheese

1 can french-fried onion
   rings

- Prepare mashed potato mix according to package directions.
- Add eggs, cheese and stir until blended.
- Spoon mixture into a lightly greased 2-quart dish. Sprinkle with onion rings.
- Bake uncovered at 325° for 25 minutes.

Potato Pancakes

3 pounds white potatoes,
  peeled, grated

1 onion, finely minced

3 eggs, beaten

½ cup seasoned dry
  breadcrumbs

• In a large bowl, combine the potatoes,
  onions, eggs, a little salt and pepper and
  breadcrumbs and mix well.

• In a skillet, drop by spoonfuls in hot oil
  and brown on both sides.

Ham Baked Potatoes

4 potatoes, baked

1 cup diced cooked ham

1 (10½ ounce) can cream
  of mushroom soup

1 cup shredded cheddar
  cheese

• Place the hot potatoes on a microwave-
  safe plate. Cut in half lengthwise.

• Fluff up the potatoes with fork. Top
  each potato with ¼ of the ham.

• In saucepan, heat the soup with ¼ cup
  water, heating just until spreadable.
  Spoon soup over potatoes and top with
  cheese.

• Microwave on high for 4 minutes or
  until hot.

Broccoli Topped Potatoes

4 hot baked potatoes,
  halved

1 cup diced, cooked ham

1 (10½ ounce) can cream
  of broccoli soup

½ cup shredded cheddar
  cheese

• Place hot baked potatoes on a microwave-safe plate.

• Carefully fluff up potatoes with fork.
  Top each potato with ham.

• Stir the soup in the can until smooth.
  Spoon soup over potatoes and top with
  cheese.

• Microwave on high for 4 minutes.

Whipped Sweet Potatoes

2 (15 ounce) cans sweet
potatoes

½ stick margarine, melted

¼ cup orange juice

1 cup miniature
marshmallows

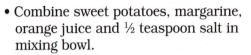

- Combine sweet potatoes, margarine, orange juice and ½ teaspoon salt in mixing bowl.
- Beat until fluffy. Fold in marshmallows.
- Spoon into a buttered 2-quart casserole.
- Bake uncovered at 350° for 25 minutes.

You might sprinkle additional marshmallows and broil until lightly browned.

Sweet Potato Casserole

1 (28 ounce) can sweet
potatoes

½ cup chopped pecans

1 ½ cups packed light
brown sugar

1 stick margarine

- Slice sweet potatoes into a two-quart casserole dish. Sprinkle pecans over sweet potatoes.
- Make a syrup of the brown sugar and margarine with just enough water to make it pourable.
- Bring to a boil and pour syrup over sweet potatoes.
- Bake at 350° for about 30 minutes until the potatoes are browned.

Sweet Potato Bake

1 (28 ounce) can sweet
potatoes, drained

1 stick margarine

1 cup packed brown
sugar

3 tart apples, peeled,
sliced

- Layer potatoes, dot with margarine and sprinkle with brown sugar; layer with apple slices.
- Repeat, ending with potatoes, margarine and brown sugar.
- Bake 30 minutes at 350° or until apples have cooked.

French Rice

1 cup uncooked rice

1 stick margarine, melted

1 can French onion soup

1 (8 ounce) can sliced
water chestnuts,
drained

- Combine rice, margarine, soup, water chestnuts and 1¼ cups water.
- Pour into a buttered 2-quart baking dish.
- Bake covered at 350° for 1 hour.

Baked Rice

2 cups uncooked rice

1 stick margarine, melted

1 (10½ ounce) can cream
of celery soup

1 (10½ ounce) can cream
of onion soup

- Combine the rice, margarine, soups and 1½ cup water.
- Pour into a buttered 3-quart baking dish.
- Bake at 350° covered for 1 hour.

Broccoli and Wild Rice

2 (10 ounce) packages
frozen chopped
broccoli

1 (6 ounce) box long grain
and wild rice

1 (8 ounce) jar Cheez
Whiz

1 (10½ ounce) can cream
of chicken soup

- Cook broccoli and rice according to package directions.
- Combine all ingredients and pour into a buttered 2-quart casserole dish.
- Bake at 350° for 25 to 30 minutes or until bubbly.

Tasty Rice

½ stick margarine

1 cup raw white rice

2 (10 ounce) cans beef broth

¼ cup parmesan cheese

- Melt margarine in a 3-quart casserole dish.
- Add the rice and pour the beef broth over rice.
- Sprinkle with parmesan cheese.
- Cover and bake at 350° for 45 minutes.

Brown Rice

1 cup rice (not instant)

1 can French onion soup

1 can beef broth

3 tablespoons margarine, melted

- Put rice in bottom of casserole dish.
- Pour soups and margarine on top.
- Bake covered at 350° for 45 minutes.

Mexican Rice

1 cup uncooked instant rice

1 green pepper, chopped

½ medium onion, chopped

2 (15 ounce) cans Mexican stewed tomatoes

- Combine all ingredients in large saucepan.
- Cover and simmer 30 minutes. Check to see if a little water needs to be added.

Mushroom Rice

1 (5.9 ounce) package chicken rice-a-roni

1 (4 ounce) can sliced mushrooms, drained

⅓ cup slivered almonds

1 (8 ounce) carton sour cream

• Prepare rice as directed on package.

• Fold in mushrooms, almonds and sour cream. Place in a 3-quart greased casserole.

• Bake covered at 350° for 25 to 30 minutes.

Green Chili Casserole

1 (7 ounce) can chopped green chilies, drained

1 pint sour cream

3 cups cooked white rice

1 (8 ounce) package shredded monterey jack cheese

• Combine all ingredients in a 2-quart baking dish.

• Cover and bake at 350° for 20 minutes.

• Uncover and bake 10 minutes longer.

Hoppin' John

4 slices bacon

1 onion, chopped

1 cup raw rice

1 (15 ounce) can black-eyed peas, undrained

• Fry bacon; drain.

• Saute onion in the bacon grease.

• In a large saucepan, combine the onion, bacon grease, salt, rice and 2½ cups water. Bring to a boil. Cover. Lower heat and simmer for 30 minutes.

• Add bacon and black-eyed peas; simmer 5 more minutes. Remove from heat and allow to stand for 5 more minutes until liquid is absorbed.

Rice 'N Beans

4 cups cooked rice

1 (15 ounce) can pinto beans, undrained

1 cup shredded cheddar cheese

3 tablespoons margarine, melted

- Mix all ingredients together in a saucepan.
- Cook over low heat until cheese is melted. Serve hot.

Easy Rice

1 onion, finely chopped

2 tablespoons margarine

1 cup raw white rice

2 (14 ounce) cans chicken broth

- Saute onion in the margarine until transparent.
- In a 2-quart casserole combine the onion, rice and broth. Cover and bake at a 350° oven for 55 minutes.

Chili Rice Bake

1 cup instant rice

1 pint sour cream

1 (7 ounce) can chopped green chilies

1 (8 ounce) package shredded Monterey Jack cheese

- Cook rice according to directions.
- Add remaining ingredients plus ½ teaspoon salt.
- Place in a buttered casserole dish.
- Bake covered at 325° for 15 to 20 minutes until thoroughly heated.

Spinach Fettuccine

1 (6 ounce) can tomato paste

1 (5 ounce) can evaporated milk

1 stick margarine or butter

1 (12 ounce) package spinach fettuccine

- In a saucepan, combine the tomato paste, milk and heat until margarine is melted.
- Season with a little salt and pepper.
- Cook fettuccine according to directions on package. Serve sauce over fettuccine.

Creamy Fettuccine

1 (8 ounce) package fettuccine

1 pound Italian sausage

1 (10½ ounce) can cream of mushroom soup

1 (16 ounce) carton sour cream

- Cook fettuccine and drain.
- Cut up sausage into 1-inch pieces and brown over medium heat cooking for about 8 minutes. Drain.
- Mix all ingredients together and place in a 2-quart greased baking dish.
- Bake at 325° for 30 minutes.

Creamy Pasta

1 (8 ounce) jar roasted red peppers, drained

1 (15 ounce) can chicken broth

1 (3 ounce) package cream cheese

8 ounces pasta

- Combine red peppers and broth in a blender, mixing well.
- Pour into a saucepan. Heat to boiling.
- Turn heat down and whisk in cream cheese. Serve over your favorite pasta.

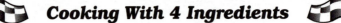
Special Macaroni and Cheese

1 (8 ounce) package small macaroni shells

1 (15 ounce) can stewed tomatoes

1 (8 ounce) package Velveeta cheese, cubed

3 tablespoons margarine, melted

• Cook shells according to package directions; drain.

• In a large bowl, combine shells, tomatoes, cheese cubes and margarine.

• Pour into a 2-quart buttered baking dish.

• Bake covered at 350° for 35 minutes.

Macaroni and Cheese

1 cup uncooked macaroni

1½ cups small curd cottage cheese

1½ cups shredded cheddar cheese or American cheese

4 tablespoons grated parmesan cheese

• Cook macaroni according to package directions; drain.

• Combine cottage cheese and both cheeses. Combine macaroni with the cheese mixture.

• Spoon into a greased 2-quart baking dish.

• Bake covered at 350° for 35 minutes.

Carnival Couscous

1 (5.7 ounce) box herbed chicken couscous

½ stick margarine

1 red bell pepper, 1 yellow squash, both cut in tiny pieces

¾ fresh broccoli flowerets, finely chopped

• Cook couscous as package directs, leaving out the butter.

• With margarine in saucepan, saute the bell pepper, squash, and broccoli, cooking about 10 minutes or until vegetables are almost tender.

• Combine couscous and vegetables. Serve hot.

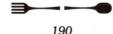

MAIN DISHES

Favorite Chicken Breasts

6-8 boneless, skinless chicken breasts

1 (10½ ounce) can golden mushroom soup

1 cup white wine or white cooking wine

1 (8 ounce) carton sour cream

- Place chicken breasts in a large, shallow baking pan. Sprinkle on a little salt and pepper. Bake uncovered at 350° for 30 minutes.
- In saucepan, combine soup, wine and sour cream; heat just enough to mix together.
- Remove chicken from oven and pour sour cream mixture over chicken. Lower heat to 300°. Return to oven to cook another 30 minutes.
- Baste twice again. Serve over rice.

Saucy Chicken

5-6 boneless, skinless chicken breasts

2 cups thick and chunky salsa

⅓ cup packed light brown sugar

1½ tablespoons dijon-style mustard

- Place chicken breasts in a greased 9 x 13-inch baking dish.
- Combine salsa, sugar and mustard and pour over chicken.
- Cover and bake at 350° for 45 minutes. Serve over rice.

Golden Chicken

6 boneless, skinless chicken breasts

½ stick margarine

1 (10½ ounce) can golden mushroom soup

½ cup sliced almonds

- Place chicken breasts in a greased 9 x 13-inch baking pan.
- In a saucepan, combine margarine, soup, almonds and ¼ cup water. Heat and mix just until margarine is melted.
- Pour mixture over chicken.
- Cover and bake at 350° for 1 hour.

Chicken and Rice

2 cups instant brown rice

2 cups cooked chicken, cut up

1 (10½ ounce) can golden mushroom soup

½ soup can milk

- Cook rice according to package directions.
- Combine rice, chicken, soup and milk; mixing well.
- Cover and bake at 350° for 30 minutes.

Chicken Crunch

4-6 boneless, skinless chicken breasts

½ cup Italian salad dressing

½ cup sour cream

2½ cups corn flakes, crushed

- Place chicken in a zip-top plastic bag; add salad dressing and sour cream. Seal, refrigerate 1 hour.
- Remove chicken from marinade, discarding marinade.
- Dredge chicken in corn flakes; place in a 9 x 13-inch non-stick sprayed baking dish.
- Bake uncovered at 375° for 45 minutes.

Chili Pepper Chicken

5 boneless, skinless chicken breasts

1 envelope hot and spicy recipe Shake'N Bake coating mixture

1 (4 ounce) can chopped green chilies

Chunky salsa

- Dredge chicken in coating mixture and place in a greased 9 x 13-inch baking dish.
- Bake at 375° for 25 minutes.
- Remove from oven and spread green chilies over the 5 chicken breasts and return to oven for 5 minutes. Serve with the salsa over each chicken breast.

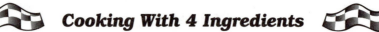

Bacon-Wrapped Chicken

6 boneless, skinless
chicken breasts

1 (8 ounce) carton
whipped cream cheese
with onion and chives,
divided

Margarine

6 bacon strips

- Flatten chicken to ½-inch thickness.
- Spread 3 tablespoons cream cheese over each. Dot with margarine and a little salt. Roll up.
- Wrap each with a bacon strip. Place seam side down in a greased 9 x 13-inch baking dish.
- Bake, uncovered at 375° for 40 to 45 minutes or until juices run clear.
- To brown, broil 6 inches from heat for about 3 minutes or until bacon is crisp.

Apricot Chicken

1 cup apricot preserves

1 (8 ounce) bottle
Catalina dressing

1 package onion soup mix

6-8 chicken breasts

- In a bowl, mix apricot preserves, dressing and soup mix.
- Place chicken breasts in a large, buttered baking dish and pour apricot mixture over chicken. (For a change of pace, use Russian dressing instead of Catalina).
- Bake uncovered at 325° for 1 hour. Serve over hot rice.

Coca Cola Chicken

4-6 boneless, skinless
chicken breasts

1 cup ketchup

1 cup Coca Cola

2 tablespoons
worcestershire sauce

- Place chicken in a 9 x 13-inch casserole dish. Sprinkle with salt and pepper.
- Mix ketchup, Coca Cola and worcestershire and pour over chicken.
- Cover and bake at 350° for 50 minutes.

Asparagus Chicken

1 package hollandaise
sauce mix

2 large boneless chicken
breasts, cut into strips

1 tablespoon lemon juice

1 (15 ounce) can
asparagus spears

- Prepare hollandaise sauce according to directions on package.
- In a large skillet with a little oil, cook chicken strips for 12 to 15 minutes or until brown, stirring occasionally.
- Add hollandaise sauce and lemon juice.
- Cover and cook another 10 minutes, stirring occasionally. Serve over hot cooked noodles. When ready to serve, place chicken strips over the noodles, then add the heated asparagus spears.

Peachy Chicken

½ cup Italian dressing

2 teaspoons ground
ginger

4 boneless, skinless
chicken breasts

⅓ cup peach preserves

- In a large plastic bag combine Italian dressing and ginger.
- Place chicken in bag and turn several times to coat chicken. Marinate in refrigerator (turning occasionally) 4 hours or overnight.
- When ready to bake remove chicken reserving ⅓ cup of the marinade.
- In a small saucepan bring reserved marinade to boil and boil for one minute. Remove from heat and stir in preserves; set aside.
- In oven broil chicken until chicken is no longer pink, brushing with preserved mixture the last 5 minutes of cooking.

Wine and Chicken

6-8 boneless, skinless chicken breasts

1 (10½ ounce) can cream of mushroom soup

1 (10½ ounce) can cream of onion soup

1 cup white wine

- In skillet brown chicken in a little bit of oil. Place in a 9 x 13-inch baking dish.
- Combine soups and wine; pour over chicken.
- Bake covered at 325° for 35 minutes.
- Uncover and bake another 25 minutes.

Baked Chicken

6 boneless, skinless chicken breasts

1 stick margarine, melted

Cornbread stuffing mix, crushed (plus seasoning)

- Dip chicken breast in melted margarine.
- Roll in cornbread stuffing mix to coat.
- Bake uncovered at 350° for 45 minutes.

Glazed Chicken and Rice

4 boneless, skinless chicken breasts, cubed

1 (20 ounce) can pineapple chunks, undrained

½ cup honey mustard grill and glaze sauce

1 red bell pepper, chopped

- In a skillet with a little oil, brown chicken and cook on low heat for 15 minutes. Add the pineapple, honey mustard and bell pepper.
- Bring to a boil, then reduce heat to low and simmer for 10 to 15 minutes or until sauce is slightly thickened.
- Serve over hot cooked rice.

Rosemary Chicken

1 tablespoon dried
  rosemary, divided

½ cup flour

Italian dressing

3-5 boneless, skinless
  chicken breasts

• Combine the flour and ½ the rosemary together.

• Place a little Italian dressing in a shallow bowl and dip chicken breasts in dressing.

• Dredge chicken in the flour mixture. Place in a 9 x 13-inch shallow baking dish.

• Bake uncovered at 350° for 40 minutes. Remove from oven and sprinkle remaining rosemary over breasts and cook another 10 minutes.

Chicken Dipping

1½ cups cornbread
  stuffing mix, plus ½ of
  the seasoning packet

4 tablespoons oil

4 boneless, skinless
  chicken breasts

Dipping Sauce

• Place stuffing mix in a plastic bag and crush with a rolling pin.

• Add oil to the center of a 9 x 13-inch baking pan and spread it around the entire pan.

• Cut chicken breasts into three or four pieces; dip in stuffing mix and place in the baking pan. Arrange chicken making sure the pieces are not touching.

• Bake at 350° uncovered for 25 minutes. Remove from oven and turn pieces over and bake another 15 minutes or until brown.

Dipping Sauce for Chicken

4 tablespoons honey

3 tablespoons spicy
  brown mustard

• To serve, dip chicken in dipping sauce and enjoy.

Lemonade Chicken

6 boneless, skinless chicken breast halves

1 (6 ounce) can frozen lemonade, thawed

⅓ cup soy sauce

1 teaspoon garlic powder

- Place chicken in a greased 9 x 13-inch baking dish.
- Combine the lemonade, soy sauce and garlic powder and pour over the chicken.
- Cover with foil and bake at 350° for 45 minutes.
- Uncover. Pour juices over chicken and cook another 10 minutes uncovered.

Classy Chicken

4 boneless, skinless chicken breasts

¼ cup lime juice

1 envelope Italian salad dressing mix

½ stick butter, melted

- Season chicken with salt and pepper; place in shallow baking dish.
- Mix lime juice, salad dressing mix and melted butter and pour over chicken.
- Cover and bake at 325° for 1 hour. Remove cover for the last 15 minutes of cooking time.

Wild Rice and Chicken

1 (6.2 ounce) package long grain and wild rice mix

4 boneless, skinless chicken breasts

4 tablespoon margarine, divided

1 large red pepper, chopped

- Prepare rice according to package directions.
- In a large skillet cook chicken in 2 tablespoons of the margarine making sure each chicken breast is browned on both sides. Remove chicken and keep warm.
- Add remaining margarine to pan drippings; saute red pepper until tender. Add to the rice. Serve with the cooked chicken breast.

Mozzarella Cutlets

4 boneless, skinless
chicken breast halves

1 cup Italian seasoned
dry breadcrumbs

1 cup prepared spaghetti
sauce

4 slices mozzarella
cheese

- Pound each chicken breast to flatten slightly.
- Coat well in breadcrumbs. Arrange chicken breasts in a greased 9 x 13-inch baking dish.
- Place ¼ of the sauce over each portion. Place slice of cheese over each and garnish with remaining breadcrumbs.
- Bake uncovered at 350° for 45 minutes.

Crispy Nutty Chicken

⅓ cup dry roasted
peanuts, minced

1 cup corn flake crumbs

½ cup ranch-style
buttermilk salad
dressing

5-6 chicken breasts

- Combine peanuts and corn flake crumbs on piece of wax paper.
- Pour salad dressing into a pie plate.
- Dip each piece of chicken in the salad dressing and roll in crumb mixture to coat.
- Arrange chicken in a 9 x 13-inch shallow baking dish.
- Bake uncovered at 350° for 50 minutes until lightly brown.

Sunday Chicken

5-6 boneless, skinless
chicken breast halves

½ cup sour cream

¼ cup soy sauce

1 (10½ ounce) can French
onion soup

- Place chicken in a greased 9 x 13-inch baking dish.
- In saucepan, combine the sour cream, soy sauce and soup; heat just enough to mix well. Pour over chicken breasts.
- Bake covered at 350° for 55 minutes.

Chicken and Beef

1 (4 ounce) jar sliced dried beef, separated

6 strips bacon

6 boneless, skinless chicken breasts

1 (10½ ounce) can cream of chicken soup

- Place dried beef in greased 9 x 13-inch baking dish.
- Wrap bacon strip around each chicken breast and place over beef.
- In a saucepan heat chicken soup and ¼ cup water just until it can be poured over chicken.
- Bake covered at 325° for 1 hour and 10 minutes.

Seasoned Chicken

4-5 boneless, skinless chicken breasts

1 tablespoon oregano

¾ teaspoon garlic powder

1 stick margarine, melted

- Place chicken breasts in a baggie and add the oregano, garlic and margarine.
- Marinate in refrigerator for 3 or 4 hours.
- Place chicken and marinade in a shallow baking dish.
- Bake covered at 325° for 1 hour.

Ritzy Chicken

6 boneless, skinless chicken breasts

½ cup sour cream

1 stack Ritz crackers, crushed into fine crumbs

¼ teaspoon pepper

- Dip chicken in sour cream and roll in cracker crumbs with pepper mixed in.
- Place chicken in a greased shallow baking dish.
- Bake uncovered at 350° for 55 minutes.

Chicken and Noodles

1 package chicken flavored instant ramen noodles

1 (16 ounce) package frozen broccoli, cauliflower and carrots

⅔ cup sweet and sour sauce

3 boneless, skinless chicken breasts, cooked, cut into thin strips

- Reserve seasoning packet from noodles. In a saucepan cook noodles and vegetables in 2 cups of boiling water for 3 minutes, stirring occasionally; drain.
- Combine noodle-vegetable mixture with seasoning packet, sweet and sour sauce and a little salt and pepper. (You may want to also add 1 tablespoon of soy sauce.)
- Add chicken and heat thoroughly.

Jiffy Chicken

8 boneless, skinless chicken breasts

¾ cup mayonnaise

2 cups crushed corn flake crumbs

½ cup grated parmesan cheese

- Sprinkle chicken breasts with salt and pepper.
- Dip chicken in mayonnaise and spread mayonnaise over chicken with a brush.
- Combine corn flakes and parmesan cheese. Dip mayonnaise-covered chicken in the cornflake mixture (get plenty of the crumbs on chicken) and place on a non-stick vegetable sprayed 9 x 13-inch glass baking dish.
- Bake uncovered at 325° for 1 hour.

Chicken Parmesan

1½ cups Rice Krispie crumbs

½ cup grated parmesan cheese

6 boneless, skinless chicken breasts

⅔ cup mayonnaise

- Combine crumbs and cheese.
- Dip chicken in the mayonnaise and coat with crumb mixture.
- Place in a greased 9 x 13- inch baking dish.
- Bake uncovered at 350° for 55 minutes.

Skillet Chicken and Stuffing

1 (6 ounce) box stuffing mix for chicken

1 (16 ounce) package frozen whole kernel corn

½ stick margarine

4 boneless, skinless chicken breast halves, cooked

- In a large skillet combine contents of the seasoning packet in the stuffing mix, corn, 1⅔ cups water and the margarine. Bring to a boil. Reduce heat, cover and simmer for 5 minutes.
- Stir in stuffing mix just until moistened.
- Cut chicken into thin slices. Mix with the stuffing-corn mixture.
- Cook on low heat just until thoroughly heated.

Chip Chicken

2 cups crushed potato chips

¼ teaspoon garlic powder

5-6 boneless, skinless chicken breasts

1 stick margarine, melted

- Mix potato chips and garlic together.
- Dip chicken breasts in margarine and then roll in potato chip mixture.
- Place in a greased shallow baking dish and bake uncovered at 350° for 55 minutes.

Chicken Dinner

1 cup rice, uncooked

6 boneless, skinless chicken breasts

1 package dry onion soup mix

1 (10 ounce) can cream of chicken soup

- Place rice in a greased 9 x 13-inch baking dish; add chicken breasts over rice.
- Combine onion soup mix, soup and 2 soup cans water. Heat just to mix well.
- Pour over chicken and rice.
- Cover and bake at 325° for 1 hour and 10 minutes.

Chicken Dijon

½ cup mayonnaise

¼ cup dijon mustard

4-5 boneless, skinless chicken breast halves

1½ cups dry breadcrumbs

- Combine the mayonnaise and mustard.
- Dip chicken in mustard mixture and dredge in the breadcrumbs.
- Place in a greased 9 x 13-inch baking dish.
- Bake uncovered at 350° for 1 hour.

Chicken Supper

5 boneless, skinless chicken breasts

5 slices onion

5 potatoes, peeled and quartered

1 (10½ ounce) can cream of celery soup

- Place chicken breasts in a 9 x 13-inch greased baking dish.
- Top chicken with onion slices, placing potatoes around chicken.
- Heat soup with ¼ cup water just enough to be able to pour the soup over chicken and vegetables.
- Bake covered at 325° for 1 hour and 10 minutes.

Ginger Chicken

2 teaspoons ground
  ginger
½ cup Italian dressing
4 boneless, skinless
  chicken breasts
⅔ cup apricot preserves

- Combine ginger and Italian dressing; place in a large baggie. Add chicken to the bag and marinate in refrigerator overnight, turning occasionally.
- When ready to cook, remove chicken, reserving ¼ cup of the marinade. Place chicken in a shallow baking dish.
- Pour the ¼ cup of marinade in saucepan, bring to a boil and cook 1 minute. Remove from heat and stir in preserves. Set aside.
- Bake chicken on 350° for 45 minutes; brush with marinade mixture the last 10 minutes of cooking.

Chicken Quesadillas

3 boneless, skinless
  chicken breasts, cubed
1 (10½ ounce) can
  cheddar cheese soup
⅔ cup chunky salsa
10 flour tortillas

- Cook chicken in skillet until juices evaporate, stirring often.
- Add soup and salsa and heat thoroughly.
- Spread about ⅓ cup soup mixture on half of each tortilla to within ½ inch of edge. Moisten edge with water, fold over and seal. Place on 2 baking sheets.
- Bake at 400° for 5 to 6 minutes.

Chicken Oriental

1 (6 ounce) jar sweet and
sour sauce

1 envelope dry onion
soup mix

1 (16 ounce) can whole
cranberry sauce

6-8 boneless, skinless
chicken breasts

- In a bowl combine the sweet and sour
sauce, onion soup mix and cranberry
sauce.

- Place chicken breasts in a Pam sprayed
9 x 13-inch shallow baking dish.

- Pour cranberry mixture over chicken
breasts.

- Bake covered at 325° for 30 minutes.
Uncover and bake 25 minutes longer.

Reuben Chicken

4 boneless, skinless
chicken breasts

4 slices Swiss cheese

1 (15 ounce) can
sauerkraut, drained

1 (8 ounce) bottle
Catalina salad dressing

- Arrange chicken breasts in a greased
shallow baking pan.

- Place cheese over chicken and then the
sauerkraut. Cover with Catalina dressing.

- Bake covered at 350° for 30 minutes.
Uncover and cook another 15 minutes.

Best Ever Meatloaf

2 pounds ground turkey

1 (6¼ ounce) package
stuffing mix for beef
plus seasoning

2 eggs, beaten

½ cup ketchup, divided

- Combine the ground turkey, stuffing
mix, eggs and ¼ cup of the ketchup.
Mix well.

- Shape meat into an oval loaf into the
center of a 9 x 13-inch baking dish.

- Spread remaining ¼ cup of ketchup on
top of loaf.

- Bake at 350° for 1 hour.

Honey Mustard Chicken

⅓ cup dijon mustard
½ cup honey
2 tablespoons dried dill
1 (2½ pound) chicken,
  quartered

- Combine mustard, honey and dill.
- Arrange chicken quarters in a 9 x 13-inch baking dish.
- Pour mustard mixture over chicken. Turn chicken over and make sure the mustard mixture covers the chicken.
- Bake covered at 350° for 35 minutes. Uncover and bake another 10 minutes.

Tangy Chicken

1 (2 pound) broiler-fryer
  chicken, cut up
3 tablespoons margarine
½ cup Heinz 57 sauce
½ cup water

- Brown chicken pieces in skillet with the margarine. Place chicken pieces in a greased shallow pan.
- Combine sauce and water; pour over chicken. Cover with foil.
- Bake at 350° for 55 minutes. Remove foil last 10 minutes of cooking time so chicken can brown.

Chicken In A Flash

1 chicken fryer, quartered
1½ cups sour cream
1 package dry onion soup
  mix
½ cup milk

- Place the 4 chicken pieces in a non-stick vegetable sprayed 9 x 13-inch baking dish.
- In a saucepan combine sour cream, onion soup mix and milk; heat just enough to mix well. Pour over chicken.
- Bake, covered at 325° for 1 hour and 15 minutes.

Onion Sweet Chicken

2 chickens, quartered
1 (15 ounce) can whole
  cranberry sauce
1 (8 ounce) bottle
  Catalina salad dressing
1 package dry onion soup
  mix

- Place chicken quarters in a well greased large shallow baking dish.
- Combine cranberry sauce, dressing and soup mix, mixing well. Pour over chicken.
- Cover and bake at 350° for 1 hour and 10 minutes. During the last 10 minutes uncover chicken and place back in oven to brown.

Sunshine Chicken

1 chicken, quartered
Flour
1 cup barbecue sauce
½ cup orange juice

- Place chicken in a bowl of flour, coating well.
- In skillet, brown chicken and place in a greased shallow baking pan.
- Combine barbecue sauce and orange juice. Pour over chicken.
- Bake covered at 350° for 45 minutes. Remove from oven and spoon sauce over chicken; bake uncovered another 20 minutes.

Company Chicken

2 chickens, quartered
2 (10½ ounce) cans cream
  of mushroom soup
1 pint sour cream
1 cup sherry

- Place chickens in a large shallow baking dish.
- In a saucepan combine soup, sour cream and sherry. Pour mixture over chicken. (You might sprinkle a little paprika on top.)
- Bake covered at 300° for 1 hour and 15 minutes.

Good served over rice.

Sweet 'N Spicy Chicken

1 pound boneless skinless chicken breasts, cut into ½-inch cubes

3 tablespoons taco seasoning

1 (11 ounce) jar chunky salsa

1 cup peach preserves

- Place the chicken in a large resealable plastic bag; add taco seasoning and toss to coat.
- In a skillet, brown the chicken in a little oil.
- Combine salsa and preserves. Stir into the skillet.
- Bring to a boil. Reduce heat and cover and simmer until the juices run clear.

Serve over rice or noodles.

Chicken Broccoli Skillet

3 cups cubed, cooked chicken

1 (16 ounce) package frozen broccoli florets

1 (8 ounce) package cubed Velveeta cheese

⅔ cup mayonnaise

- In a skillet, combine the chicken, broccoli, cheese and ¼ cup water. Cover and cook over medium heat until broccoli is crisp-tender and cheese is melted.
- Stir in mayonnaise; heat through, but do not boil.

Serve over hot cooked rice.

Chicken Cacciatore

3 chicken breasts, 3 chicken thighs

1 onion, chopped

1 (26 ounce) jar spaghetti sauce

1 teaspoon dried basil

- Brown chicken pieces in a little oil or margarine. Remove chicken to a separate plate and saute onion in the same skillet.
- Place chicken back in skillet and pour spaghetti sauce over chicken and onions, adding the basil.
- Cover and simmer about 30 minutes.

Serve over spaghetti.

Fajitas in a Flash

2 cups leftover chicken or turkey, chopped very fine

8 (8-inch) flour tortillas

¾-1 cup chunky salsa

¾-1 cup shredded cheddar cheese

- The chicken needs to be chopped up very fine, almost to being grated. Season with a little seasoned salt and pepper.
- Lay all tortillas out on waxed paper. Spread the chicken down center of each tortilla. Top with salsa and cheese.
- Roll tortillas up, using a toothpick to hold together.
- Place on a cookie sheet; heat at 300° for about 10 to 15 minutes – not to cook, just to warm. Serve with extra salsa.

Italian Chicken and Rice

3 boneless chicken breasts, cut into strips

1 (14 ounce) can chicken broth seasoned with Italian herbs

¾ cup uncooked rice

¼ cup grated parmesan cheese

- Cook chicken in a non-stick skillet until brown, stirring often. Remove chicken.
- To the skillet add the broth and rice. Heat to boiling point.
- Cover and simmer over low heat for 25 minutes (check to see if it needs more water).
- Stir in cheese. Return chicken to pan.
- Cover and cook for 5 minutes or until done.

Sweet and Sour Chicken

2-3 pounds chicken pieces

Oil

1 package dry onion soup mix

1 (6 ounce) can frozen orange juice concentrate, thawed

- In a skillet, brown chicken in a little oil. Place chicken in a 9 x 13-inch baking dish.
- In a small bowl, combine onion soup mix, orange juice and ⅔ cup water, stirring well. Pour over chicken.
- Bake uncovered at 350° for 50 minutes.

Curried Chicken Casserole

1 (10 ounce) box chicken flavor Rice a Roni

2 (5 ounce) cans chunk white chicken, undrained

1 teaspoon curry powder

⅓ cup raisins (optional)

- In a skillet, prepare the Rice a Roni according to the directions on the box.
- Once the Rice a Roni is cooked, add curry powder and chicken plus liquid and raisins; mix well.
- Cover and remove from heat. Let stand 10 minutes and serve.

El Pronto Chicken

4 boneless, skinless chicken breasts

1 stick butter, melted

⅔ cup seasoned breadcrumbs

½ cup grated parmesan cheese

- Dip chicken in the butter.
- Mix together the crumbs, cheese, some garlic powder, salt and pepper.
- Roll chicken in crumb-cheese mixture. Place in a greased 9 x 13-inch baking dish.
- Cover and bake at 350° for 55 minutes.

Serve over a bed of rice.

E Z Chicken

6-8 boneless, skinless chicken breasts

1 (10½ ounce) can cream of chicken soup

1 (3 ounce) package cream cheese

1 (8 ounce) carton sour cream

- Place chicken breast in a 9 x 13-inch shallow baking dish.
- In saucepan, combine soup, cream cheese, and sour cream. Heat on low just until cream cheese is melted and all three are mixed well.
- Pour mixture over chicken breasts and sprinkle chicken breasts with lemon pepper.
- Cover and bake at 300° for 60 minutes. Uncover and bake another 15 minutes.

Serve over cooked rice.

Turkey Casserole

1 (7 ounce) package herb seasoned stuffing

1 cup whole cranberry sauce

1 (12 ounce) can turkey

1 (10 ounce) can turkey gravy

- Prepare stuffing according to package directions.
- In medium bowl combine the prepared stuffing and cranberry sauce; set aside.
- In a buttered, 2-quart baking dish place the turkey. Pour gravy over the turkey and spoon stuffing mixture over casserole.
- Bake uncovered at 375° for 15 to 20 minutes or until hot and bubbly.

Chicken for Lunch

4 cooked chicken breast
slices from deli (thick
sliced)

1 (3 ounce) package
cream cheese, softened

3 tablespoons salsa

2 tablespoons
mayonnaise

• Place chicken slices on serving platter.

• With mixer, cream together the cream
cheese, salsa and mayonnaise. Place a
heaping tablespoon on top of chicken
slices.

Serve cold.

Wings Parmesan

10 chicken wings

1 stick margarine, melted

⅓ cup parmesan cheese,
1 teaspoon garlic
powder

½ cup seasoned
breadcrumbs

• Dip wings in margarine and then in
combined mixture of cheese, garlic
powder and breadcrumbs.

• Place in casserole dish and bake at 325°
for one hour.

Turkey and Noodles

2½ cups diced cooked
turkey

1 (8 ounce) package
noodles

1 package chicken gravy,
prepared

2 cups Ritz cracker
crumbs

• Boil noodles according to directions on
package; drain.

• Arrange alternate layers of noodles,
turkey and gravy in greased 2-quart
baking dish. Cover with crumbs.

• Bake uncovered at 350° for 35 minutes.

Cornish Game Hens

4 Cornish game hens

4 tablespoons margarine

½ cup water

2 tablespoons soy sauce

- Rub hens with margarine.
- Place in greased baking dish and spoon water and soy sauce mixture over hens.
- Cover with foil and bake at 350° for 45 minutes.
- Remove cover and bake 15 minutes longer.

Duck with Cherry Sauce

1 (4-5 pound) domestic duckling

1 (12 ounce) jar cherry preserves

2 tablespoons red wine vinegar

- Prick skin of duckling. Place breast side down on a rack in a shallow roasting pan.
- Bake uncovered at 325° for 2 hours or when a meat thermometer reads 180°. Drain fat from the pan.
- Cover and let stand for 20 minutes before carving.

For the sauce combine, preserves and vinegar in a small saucepan. Heat and stir over medium heat until heated through. Serve with the duck.

Smothered Steak

1 large round steak

1 (10½ ounce) can golden mushroom soup

1 envelope dry onion soup mix

⅔ cup milk

• Cut steak into serving-size pieces and place in a well greased 9 x 13-inch baking pan.

• In a saucepan mix soup, dry onion soup and milk. Heat just enough to be able to mix well. Pour over steak.

• Seal with foil. Bake at 325° for 1 hour.

Swiss Steak

1½ pounds round steak

½ teaspoon seasoned salt

½ teaspoon garlic powder

2 (15 ounce) cans stewed tomatoes, divided

• Season steak with seasoned salt and garlic powder. Dip in flour and brown in a little oil or margarine.

• Pour one can tomatoes into a 9 x 13-inch baking dish. Place steak over tomatoes and pour remaining can of tomatoes over steak.

• Cover and bake 1½ hours at 325°.

Roasted Garlic Steak

2 (15 ounce) cans tomato with roasted garlic and herb soup

½ cup Italian salad dressing

⅓ cup water

1½ pounds (¾-inch) boneless beef sirloin steak

• In saucepan, combine soups, dressing and water.

• Broil steaks to desired doneness; allow 15 minutes for medium. Turn once and brush often with the sauce.

• Heat remaining sauce to serve with steak.

Flank Steak

2-3 pounds flank steak

1 (8 ounce) bottle Italian salad dressing

Seasoned salt

1 (4 ounce) can sliced mushrooms

- Marinate steak in salad dressing for 8 hours. Remove from marinade. Sprinkle with seasoning salt.
- Broil 10 minutes on each side.
- Slice steak very thin.
- Heat mushrooms and place around steak.

Steak and Mushrooms

1½ pounds round steak, cut in strips

1 package dry onion soup mix

1 (4 ounce) can sliced mushrooms, undrained

1 (8 ounce) carton sour cream

- In a large skillet, brown the strips of steak; add soup mix and ¾ cup water.
- Simmer for about 20 minutes or until liquid is about cooked out.
- Add mushrooms and sour cream.
- Heat thoroughly.

Serve over noodles.

Baked Steak

1½ pounds round steak, (½ thick)

Salt and pepper

1 (10½ ounce) can cream of mushroom soup

1 envelope dry onion soup mix

- Place steak in a greased 9 x 13-inch baking dish. Sprinkle with salt and pepper.
- Pour mushroom soup and ½ cup water over steak and sprinkle with onion soup mix.
- Cover and bake at 325° for 2 hours.

Mushroom Round Steak

2 pounds (¾-inch thick) round steak

1 package dry onion soup mix

1 cup dry red wine

1 (4 ounce) can sliced mushrooms

- Remove all fat from steak and cut in serving size pieces. Brown meat in skillet with a little oil on both sides. Place steak in a buttered 9 x 13-inch casserole dish.

- In a frying pan combine the onion soup mix, wine, 1 cup hot water and mushrooms. Pour over browned steak.

- Cover and bake for 1 hour 20 minutes or until steak is tender.

Round Steak

2 pounds (½-inch thick) round steak

Flour, oil

2 (10½ ounce) cans tomato bisque soup

1 onion, thinly sliced

- Cut steak into serving size pieces. Dust with flour and a little salt and pepper. In a skillet brown meat in a little oil.

- Mix onions and soup with 1 can water and add to steak. Bring to boil.

- Turn heat down and simmer for 1 hour 20 minutes.

Pot Roast

1 (4-6 pound) chuck roast

1 package dry onion soup mix

1 (10½ ounce) can French onion soup

4-6 potatoes, peeled and quartered

- Place roast on large sheet of heavy duty foil.

- Mix soups and cover roast with soup mixture.

- Add potatoes and secure edges tightly.

- Bake about 3 to 4 hours at 350°.

Pepper Steak

Seasoning salt

1 (1¼ pound) sirloin steak, cut into strips

1 (16 ounce) package frozen bell pepper and onion strips, thawed

1 (1 pound) box Mexican Velveeta cheese, cut up

• Sprinkle steak with seasoned salt.

• Coat large skillet with non-stick vegetable spray. Cook steak strips about 10 minutes or until no longer pink. Remove steak from skillet and set aside.

• Stir in vegetables and ½ cup water. Simmer vegetables about 5 minutes until all liquid is cooked out.

• Add the Velveeta cheese. Turn heat to medium low until cheese is melted. Stir in steak and serve over hot cooked rice.

Eye of Round

½ teaspoon seasoned salt

½ teaspoon garlic powder

1 teaspoon ground oregano

1 (6 pound) eye of round roast

• Combine seasoned salt, garlic and oregano. Sprinkle over roast.

• Place in shallow baking pan with fat side up.

• Bake at 350° for 2½ to 3 hours.

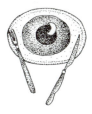

Beef and Noodles

3 pounds lean beef, cubed

2 (10½ ounce) cans golden mushroom soup

½ cup cooking sherry

1 package dry onion soup mix

• Mix all ingredients adding ¾ cup water. Pour into a 3-quart baking dish.

• Bake at 325° for about 2 hours. *Serve over noodles.*

Easy Roast

1 (4 pound) rump roast

1 (10½ ounce) can cream of mushroom soup

1 envelope dry onion soup mix

½ cup white wine

- Place roast in roaster.
- Combine mushroom soup, onion soup mix and white wine and ⅓ cup water. Pour over roast.
- Cover roast with foil and bake at 325° for about 3 to 4 hours.

Pot Roast and Gravy

1 (3-4 pound) rump roast

1 package dry onion soup mix

1 (10½ ounce) can golden mushroom soup

1 soup can water

- Place roast in a roaster; sprinkle dry onion soup mix over roast and cover with mushroom soup.
- Completely seal roast with the lid over foil.
- Bake at 350° for 3 to 3½ hours. Gravy will be in pan.

Rump Roast

1 (3-4 pound) boneless rump roast

4 medium potatoes, peeled, cut into pieces

2 onions, quartered

1 (10½ ounce) can golden mushroom soup

- Place roast in a roaster; season with seasoned salt and pepper, cover.
- Bake at 350° for about 1 hour.
- Uncover; add potatoes and onions. Continue cooking for another hour.
- In a saucepan combine soup and ½ cup water; heat just to be able to pour over roast and vegetables.
- Place roaster back in oven just until soup is hot.

Easy Salisbury Steak

1¼ pounds lean ground beef

½ cup flour

1 egg

1 (10 ounce) can beef gravy

- In a large bowl, combine beef, flour and egg. Add a little seasoned salt and pepper; mix well.
- Shape into 5 patties and place in a shallow 7 x 11-inch baking dish.
- Bake uncovered at 350° for 20 minutes; drain off any fat.
- Pour beef gravy over patties. Bake another 20 minutes.

Serve with rice or noodles.

Onion Beef Bake

3 pounds lean ground beef

1 package dry onion soup mix

½ cup water

2 (10½ ounce) cans condensed French onion soup

- Combine beef, soup mix and water. Stir well and shape into patties about ½-inch thick.
- Cook in a large skillet and brown on both sides.
- Move patties to a 9 x 13-inch baking dish. Pour the soup over the patties.
- Cover and bake at 350° for about 35 minutes.

A Wicked Meatloaf

1 (7 ounce) package stuffing mix, plus seasoning packet

1 egg

½ cup salsa

1½ pounds lean ground beef

- In a bowl combine stuffing mix, seasoning, egg, salsa and ⅓ cup water; mix well.
- Add ground beef to the stuffing mixture.
- Spoon into a 9 x 5-inch loaf pan.
- Bake at 350° for 1 hour.

Tater Tots and Beef

2 pounds extra lean
  ground beef

2 (10½ ounce) cans
  golden mushroom soup

1 cup grated cheddar
  cheese

1 (2 pound) package
  frozen tater tots

- Pat ground beef in bottom of greased 9 x 13-inch pan.
- Spread soup over meat and cover with grated cheese. Top with tater tots.
- Bake covered for 1 hour at 350°. Uncover for the last 15 minutes.

Potato Bake

1 pound ground beef

1 can sloppy joe sauce

1 (10½ ounce) can fiesta
  nacho cheese soup

1 (32 ounce) package
  frozen hash browned
  potatoes, thawed

- In a skillet cook beef over medium heat until no longer pink; drain.
- Add sloppy joe sauce and fiesta nacho cheese soup.
- Place hash browns in a greased 9 x 13-inch baking dish. Top with the beef mixture.
- Cover and bake at 400° for 25 minutes. Uncover and bake 10 minutes longer.

This is good sprinkled with a cup of grated cheddar cheese.

Beef Patties

1 pound lean ground beef

1 egg

1 onion, chopped

1 (15 ounce) can beef broth

- Mix beef, egg and onion. Shape into patties and brown over high heat, drain off any fat.
- Pour beef broth over patties..
- Simmer uncovered until liquid is about cooked out.

Beef Loaf

1 pound ground round
  beef, browned

1 (10½ ounce) can each
  cream of mushroom
  soup and cream of
  celery soup

1 package dry onion soup
  (savory herb with
  garlic) mix

1 cup cooked rice

- Mix all ingredients together.
- Place into a 9 x 13-inch baking dish
  and form a loaf.
- Bake at 350° for 50 minutes.

Barbecue In A Muffin

1 pound lean ground beef

⅔ cup barbecue sauce

1 (10 biscuit) can
  refrigerator biscuits

¾ cup grated cheddar
  cheese

- Brown meat, drain.
- Add barbeque sauce and simmer 15
  minutes.
- Place biscuits in greased muffin tins,
  pressing dough up sides of edge of cup.
  Spoon meat mixture into cups.
  Sprinkle with cheese.
- Bake at 350° for 12 to 15 minutes.

Beef Patties Supreme

1 pound lean ground beef

1 cup leftover mashed
  potatoes or instant

2 tablespoons minced
  onion

1 teaspoon seasoned salt

- Mix beef, potatoes, onion, seasoned salt
  and ½ teaspoon black pepper. Form
  into patties.
- Place a little oil in skillet.
- Brown and cook until all pink is gone
  from beef.

Beef and Shells

1¼ pounds lean ground beef

1 onion, chopped

1 (10½ ounce) can cream of celery soup

1 package Velveeta shells and cheese

- In a skillet, brown beef and onion, stirring until beef is crumbly.
- Add a little black pepper and garlic salt. Add soup and mix.
- Prepare shells and cheese according to package directions. Stir into beef mixture.
- Simmer about 20 minutes. Serve hot.

Cheeseburger Pasta

1 pound lean ground beef

1 (10½ ounce) can cheddar cheese soup

1 (10½ ounce) can tomato bisque soup

2 cups uncooked shell pasta

- In skillet cook beef until brown, drain fat.
- Add the soups, 1½ cups water and the pasta. Bring to a boil.
- Cover and cook over medium heat 10 to 12 minutes or until pasta is done, stirring often.

Oven Brisket

1 (5-6 pound) trimmed brisket

1 package dry onion soup mix

1 (12 ounce) can Coca Cola (not diet)

1 (10 ounce) bottle Heinz 57 sauce

- Place brisket, fat side up, in a roasting pan. In a bowl, combine onion mix, Coca Cola and Heinz 57 sauce. Pour over brisket.

- Cover and cook at 325° for 4 to 5 hours or until tender.

- Remove brisket from pan and pour off drippings. Chill both, separately, overnight.

- The next day, trim all the fat from meat, slice and reheat. Skim the fat off the drippings and reheat; serve sauce over the brisket.

Easy Brisket

1 (4-5 pound) brisket

1 envelope dry onion soup mix

2 tablespoons worcestershire

1 cup red wine

- Place brisket in a shallow baking pan.
- Sprinkle onion soup over the brisket.
- Pour worcestershire and red wine in the pan.
- Cover and bake at 325° for 5 to 6 hours.

Barbecue Brisket

½ cup liquid hickory-
flavored smoke

1 (4-5 pound) beef brisket

1 (5 ounce) bottle
worcestershire

¾ cup barbecue sauce

- Pour liquid smoke over brisket. Cover and refrigerate overnight.
- Drain. Pour worcestershire sauce over brisket.
- Cover and bake at 275° for 6 to 7 hours.
- Cover with barbeque sauce. Bake uncovered for another 30 minutes. Slice very thin across the grain.

Corned Beef Supper

1 (4-5 pound) corned beef
brisket

4 large potatoes, peeled,
quartered

6 carrots, peeled, halved

1 head cabbage

- Place corned beef in roaster, cover with water. Bring to a boil. Turn heat down and simmer 3 hours, adding water if necessary.
- Add potatoes and carrots. Cut cabbage into eighths and lay over top of other vegetables.
- Bring to a boil; turn heat down and cook another 30 to 40 minutes, until vegetables are done. When slightly cool, slice corned beef across the grain.

Mexican Supper

1 dozen tamales

1 (15 ounce) can chili,
without beans

1 (8 ounce) package
shredded cheddar
cheese

1 cup chopped onions

- Remove wrappers from tamales and place in greased 9 x 13-inch baking dish.
- Top with chili and sprinkle with cheese and onions.
- Bake for 25 minutes at 350°.

Corned Beef

1 (5 pound) corned beef
   brisket

Whole cloves

½ cup maple syrup

¼ teaspoon black pepper

- Place corned beef in a casserole with water to cover beef. Bring to boil. Lower the heat and simmer until done, allowing 50 minutes per pound.
- When corned beef has cooked, place on a rack in a shallow pan. Stick the whole cloves in a crosswise design.
- Pour syrup over meat and sprinkle with black pepper.
- Place in oven at 375° to brown and glaze for about 15 minutes. When ready to serve, slice beef across the grain. Serve hot or at room temperature.

Serve with creamed cabbage.

Cheese 'N Wiener Crescents

8 large wieners

4 slices American cheese,
   cut into 6 strips each

1 (8 ounce) can
   refrigerated crescent
   dinner rolls

- Slit wieners to within ½-inch of end; insert 3 strips of cheese in each slit.
- Separate crescent dough into 8 triangles; wrap dough over wiener keeping cheese side up. Place on cookie sheet.
- Bake at 375° for 12 to 15 minutes or until golden brown.

Kids' Stew

1 package beef hot dogs	• Cut hot dogs in ½-inch pieces.
2 potatoes, peeled and diced	• In a skillet with a little oil, brown hot dogs and diced potatoes.
2 tablespoons flour	• Mix flour and ½ cup water; pour over hot dog and potato mixture. Sprinkle with the seasoned salt.
½ teaspoon seasoned salt	
	• Cover and simmer until potatoes are done.

Chihuahua Dogs

1 (10 ounce) can chili hot dog sauce	• Put hot dog sauce in a saucepan.
1 package 10 frankfurters	• Place a frank in each taco shell. Top with the heated chili sauce and cheese; onions and tomatoes if you like.
10 preformed taco shells	
Shredded cheddar cheese	• Place in microwave and heat for 30 seconds or until the frankfurters are warm.

Stroganoff Stew

1 package dry onion soup mix

2 (10½ ounce) cans golden mushroom soup

2 pounds stew meat

1 (8 ounce) carton sour cream

• Combine onion soup mix, mushroom soup and 1 can water. Pour over stew meat.

• Cover tightly. Bake at 275° for 6 to 8 hours.

• When ready to serve, stir in sour cream. Return mixture to oven until heated thoroughly.

Serve over noodles.

Texas Chili Pie

2 (20 ounce) cans chili without beans

1 (16 ounce) package small Fritos

1 onion, chopped

1 (16 ounce) package shredded cheddar cheese

• Heat chili in saucepan.

• In 9 x 13-inch baking dish, layer the Fritos, chili, onion and cheese ⅓ at a time. Repeat layers with cheese on top.

• Bake at 325° for 20 minutes or until cheese bubbles.

Honey Spiced Pork Chops

6 pork chops
¼ cup soy sauce
¼ cup chili sauce
½ cup honey

- Place pork chops in a greased 9 x 13-inch baking pan.
- In a small bowl, combine the soy sauce, chili sauce and honey. Pour mixture over pork chops.
- Cover and bake at 325° for about 55 minutes.

Pork Chops in Cream Gravy

4 (¼-inch thick) pork chops
Flour
Oil
2¼ cups whole milk

- Trim all fat off pork chops. Dip chops in flour with a little salt and pepper.
- Brown pork chops on both sides in a little oil. Remove chops from skillet.
- Add about 2 tablespoons flour to skillet and brown lightly; stir in a little salt and pepper. Slowly stir in milk to make gravy. Return chops to skillet with the gravy.
- Cover and simmer on low burner for about 40 minutes.

Serve over rice or noodles.

Skillet Dinner

6-8 thick, boneless pork chops
2 tablespoons oil
1 box scalloped potatoes
Milk

- In skillet, brown chops in oil. Remove chops and set aside.
- Pour potatoes and packet of seasoned sauce mix into skillet. Stir in water and milk called for on package.
- Heat to boiling, reduce heat and place pork chops on top. Cover and simmer about 45 minutes.

Cranberries and Pork Chops

6-8 thick pork chops

Flour

2 cups fresh or frozen
   cranberries

1 cup sugar

- Coat the pork chops in flour; brown in a small amount of oil in skillet. Place in a shallow baking dish.
- Add the cranberries, sugar and ½ cup water.
- Cover. Bake at 350° for 30 minutes. Uncover and continue baking for another 30 minutes.

Mexicali Pork Chops

1 envelope taco seasoning

4 (½-inch thick) boneless
   pork loin chops

1 tablespoon oil

Salsa

- Rub taco seasoning over pork chops.
- In a skillet, brown pork chops in oil over medium heat.
- Add 2 tablespoons water; turn heat to low and simmer pork chops about 40 minutes. Check to see if a little more water is needed.
- Spoon salsa over pork chops to serve.

Chops and Stuffing

1 (6 ounce) box savory
   herb stuffing mix

6 center cut pork chops

Oil

3 onions, halved

- Make stuffing according to package directions and set aside.
- Fry pork chops in skillet with a little oil. Brown chops on both sides and place in a greased 9 x 13-inch baking dish.
- Divide stuffing and onions among pork chops and mound on top of each.
- Cover and bake at 350° for about 30 minutes.

Apple Pork Chops

4 butterflied pork chops

2 apples, peeled and cored

2 teaspoons margarine

2 tablespoons brown
   sugar

- Place pork chops in a non-stick sprayed shallow baking dish. Season with salt and pepper.
- Cover and bake at 350° for 30 minutes.
- Uncover, and place apple halves on top of pork chops. Add a little butter and a little brown sugar on each of these apples.
- Bake for another 15 minutes.

Pork Casserole

4-5 potatoes, peeled and
   sliced

6 pork chops

1 (10½ ounce) can fiesta
   nacho cheese soup

½ can milk

- Place two layers of potatoes in bottom of a greased casserole dish. Place pork chops on top.
- Combine cheese and milk. Heat just enough to be poured. Pour over chops.
- Bake covered at 350° for 45 minutes. Uncover and bake another 15 minutes.

Baked Pork Chops

¾ cup ketchup

¾ cup packed brown
   sugar

¼ cup lemon juice

4 butterflied pork chops

- Combine ketchup, ½ cup water, brown sugar and lemon juice.
- Place pork chops in a 7 x 11-inch buttered baking dish and pour sauce over pork chops.
- Bake covered at 325° for 50 minutes.

Spicy Pork Chops

4-6 pork chops

1 large onion

1 bell pepper

1 (10 ounce) can diced tomatoes and green chilies

- Brown pork chops in a skillet with a little oil.
- Spray casserole dish with non-stick spray. Place chops in dish.
- Cut onion and bell pepper into large chunks and place on chops. Pour tomato and green chilies over chops; sprinkle 1 teaspoon salt over casserole.
- Bake covered at 350° for 45 minutes.

Pork Chop Dinner

4 medium potatoes, peeled

2 large onions, sliced

4-6 medium thick pork chops

Milk

- Peel and thinly slice potatoes and onions.
- Place a layer of potatoes in the bottom of a 9 x 13-inch baking dish, sprinkle with salt and pepper. Place a layer of onions in dish and sprinkle with salt and pepper.
- Arrange pork chops on top, sprinkle with salt and pepper.
- Carefully pour the milk into dish until it is about ½-inch deep. Cover dish with foil sealing around edges.
- Bake covered at 325° for 1 hour. Uncover and bake 15 minutes more to brown chops.

Sweet and Sour Spareribs

4 pounds pork spareribs

1 (6 ounce) can lemonade concentrate

½ teaspoon garlic salt

⅓ cup soy sauce

- Place ribs, meaty side down in a shallow roasting pan. Cook covered at 350° for 40 minutes.
- Remove cover, drain fat and return ribs to oven. Bake 30 minutes more. Drain fat again.
- Combine remaining ingredients and brush on ribs.
- Reduce temperature to 325°. Cover and bake for 1 more hour or until tender, brushing occasionally with sauce.

Saucy Pork Chops

4 (½-inch thick) pork chops

1 tablespoon oil

1 can cream of onion soup

2 tablespoons soy sauce

- In skillet, brown pork chops in oil and cook about 15 minutes; drain.
- Add soup and soy sauce. Heat to a boil.
- Return chops to pan. Reduce heat to low. Cover and simmer about 20 minutes.

Cranberry Ham

1 (1-inch thick) slice ham

1 cup whole cranberry sauce

¼ cup packed brown sugar

⅓ teaspoon ground cloves

- Place ham in greased shallow pan.
- Spoon cranberry sauce evenly over ham.
- Sprinkle with brown sugar and cloves.
- Bake covered at 325° for about 45 minutes.

Honey Ham Slice

⅓ cup orange juice

⅓ cup honey

1 teaspoon prepared
  mustard

1 (1-inch thick) slice fully
  cooked ham

- Combine orange juice, honey and mustard in a saucepan and cook slowly for 10 minutes, stirring occasionally.
- Place ham in a broiling pan about 3 inches from heat. Brush with orange glaze.
- Broil 8 minutes on first side. Turn ham slice over. Brush with glaze again and broil another 6 to 8 minutes.

Orange Pork Chops

6-8 medium thick pork
  chops

½ stick margarine

2¼ cups orange juice

2 tablespoons orange
  marmalade

- Brown both sides of pork chops in margarine in hot skillet adding salt and pepper.
- Pour orange juice over chops. Cover and simmer until done about one hour but time will vary with the thickness of the pork chops. Add more orange juice if necessary.
- During the last few minutes of cooking add the 2 tablespoons of orange marmalade.

This makes a delicious gravy to serve over rice.

Hawaiian Pork

2 pound lean pork tenderloin, cut in 1-inch cubes

1 (15 ounce) can pineapple chunks, undrained

1 (12 ounce) bottle chili sauce

1 teaspoon ground ginger

- In skillet, season pork cubes with salt and pepper.
- Combine meat, pineapple with juice, chili sauce and ginger.
- Simmer covered for 1½ hours.

Serve over rice.

Sunday Ham

2-3 pounds boneless smoked ham

¼ cup prepared mustard

¼ cup packed brown sugar

4 potatoes, peeled, quartered

- Place ham in roaster.
- Combine mustard and sugar. Spread over ham.
- Place potatoes around ham.
- Cover and bake at 300° for 2½ to 3 hours.

Mustard Ham

1 (1-inch) slice of cooked ham

2 teaspoons dry mustard

⅓ cup honey

⅓ cup cooking wine

- Rub ham slice with the dry mustard, using 1 teaspoon mustard for each side. Place in a shallow baking pan.
- Combine honey and wine; pour over ham.
- Bake uncovered at 350° for about 35 minutes.

Supper in a Dish

2 bags instant rice in a bag

1½ cups cubed, cooked ham

1½ cups shredded cheddar cheese

1 (8 ounce) can green peas

- Prepare rice according to directions on package.
- In a large bowl, combine rice, ham, cheese and peas.
- Pour into a 3-quart baking dish and bake at 350° for 15 to 20 minutes.

Ham and Veggies

2 (16 ounce) packages mixed vegetables

1 (10½ ounce) can cream of celery soup

2 cups cubed, cooked ham

½ teaspoon dried basil

- Cook vegetables as directed on package.
- Add soup, ham and basil.
- Cook until thoroughly heated. Serve hot.

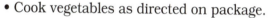

Ham Patties

2 cups ground ham (use leftover ham)

2 eggs, slightly beaten

1 cup cracker crumbs

- Combine ham, eggs, cracker crumbs and a little pepper. Shape into patties.
- Place a little oil in a heavy skillet and saute patties until golden brown.

Cranberry Sauce

1 (14 ounce) carton
strawberry glaze

1 (12 ounce) package
frozen cranberries

½ cup orange juice

Sugar

- In saucepan combine the glaze, cranberries and juice. Heat to boiling.
- Reduce heat and simmer 10 minutes or until cranberries pop, stirring often.
- Refrigerate several hours before serving.
- Cool and taste. Add sugar if necessary. *Serve with pork or ham.*

Glazed Ham

1 cup strawberry glaze

1 cup sugar

¼ teaspoon cinnamon

1 (20 ounce) can apple pie
filling

- In saucepan combine glaze, sugar and cinnamon. Heat on low.
- Stir in pie filling.
- Heat, stirring constantly so glaze will not burn.
- Spoon over cooked ham slices.

Spunky Spareribs

5-6 pounds spareribs

1 (6 ounce) can frozen
orange juice, undiluted

2 teaspoons
worcestershire sauce

½ teaspoon garlic powder

- Place spareribs in a shallow baking pan, meaty side down. Sprinkle with a little salt and pepper.
- Roast at 375° for 30 minutes.
- Turn ribs and roast another 30 minutes. Drain off fat.
- Combine remaining ingredients and brush the mixture on ribs.
- Reduce heat to 300°. Cover ribs and roast 2 hours or until tender, basting occasionally.

Spareribs With Sauerkraut

2 (15 ounce) cans
sauerkraut

¼ cup packed brown
sugar

4 pounds spareribs

½ cup hot water

- Place sauerkraut in greased casserole and sprinkle with brown sugar.
- Place spareribs on sauerkraut.
- Add hot water, cover and bake at 325° for 2½ hours or until tender.

Barbecued Spareribs

3-4 pounds pork
spareribs

2 medium onions, sliced

1 (12 ounce) bottle
barbecue sauce

½ cup packed brown
sugar

- Place ribs in roaster; add onions.
- Combine barbecue sauce and brown sugar and pour sauce over ribs.
- Cook covered at 325° for 1½ hours. Remove cover and cook 30 minutes longer.

Orange Spareribs

4-5 pounds pork
spareribs

1 (6 ounce) can orange
juice concentrate,
thawed

½ teaspoon garlic salt

⅔ cup honey

- Place ribs, meaty side down in a shallow roasting pan. Bake at 350° for 30 minutes.
- Drain off fat and turn ribs. Bake 30 minutes more.
- Combine remaining ingredients and brush on ribs.
- Reduce temperature to 325°. Cover pan and bake 1½ hours or until tender, brushing with sauce several times.

Tequila Baby Back Ribs

4 pounds baby back pork ribs

1 (12 ounce) bottle tequila lime marinade, divided

Black pepper

- Cut ribs in lengths to fit in large, resealable plastic bag.
- Place ribs in bag and add ¾ cup marinade; seal bag and shake to coat. Marinate in refrigerator overnight. Place ribs in a shallow baking dish coated with non-stick vegetable spray; discard used marinade.
- Cover ribs with foil and bake at 375° for 30 minutes.
- Remove from oven and spread a little of the extra marinade over ribs. Lower heat to 300° and cook for 1 hour.
- Uncover to let ribs brown; bake 30 minutes longer.

Plum Peachy Pork Roast

1 (4-5 pound) boneless pork loin roast

1 (12 ounce) jar plum jelly

½ cup peach preserves

½ teaspoon ginger

- Place roast in a shallow baking pan and bake at 325° for about 35 minutes. Turn roast to brown the other side and bake another 35 minutes.
- In a saucepan heat the jelly, peach preserves and ginger.
- When roast is finished cooking brush roast generously with preserve mixture.
- Bake and baste another 15 minutes.

Pork Tenderloin

3 pounds pork tenderloin

1 (15 ounce) can stewed tomatoes

1 package savory herb with garlic soup mix

2 tablespoons worcestershire sauce

- Place tenderloin strips in roaster.
- Mix remaining ingredients; spread over meat.
- Bake covered at 325° for 1 hour and 20 minutes.

Tenderloin With Apricot Sauce

3 pounds pork tenderloin

1 cup apricot preserves

⅓ cup lemon juice, ⅓ cup ketchup

1 tablespoon soy sauce

- Place tenderloins in roaster.
- Combine preserves, lemon juice, ketchup and soy sauce.
- Pour over pork and bake covered at 325° for one hour and 20 minutes. Baste once during cooking.

Serve over white rice.

Pork Picante

1 pound pork tenderloin, cubed

2 tablespoons taco seasoning

1 cup chunky salsa

⅓ cup peach preserves

- Toss pork with the taco seasoning and brown with a little oil in a skillet.
- Stir in salsa and preserves. Bring to a boil.
- Lower heat and simmer 30 minutes.

Pour over hot cooked rice.

Apple Topped Tenderloin

1½ cups hickory
marinade, divided

1 (3-4 pound) pork
tenderloin

1 (20 ounce) can apple pie
filling

¾ teaspoon cinnamon

• In a baggie combine 1 cup marinade
and tenderloin; seal bag. Marinade in
refrigerator for at least 1 hour.

• Remove tenderloin; discard used marinade.

• Cook tenderloin uncovered at 325° for 1
hour, basting twice with ¼ cup of the
marinade. Let stand 10 or 15 minutes
before slicing. In a saucepan combine
pie filling, the extra ¼ cup marinade
and cinnamon; heat.

*Serve heated apples over sliced
tenderloin.*

Italian Sausage and Ravioli

1 pound sweet Italian
pork sausage, casing
removed

1 (1 pound, 10 ounce) jar
extra chunky
mushroom and green
pepper spaghetti sauce

1 (24 ounce) package
frozen cheese-filled
ravioli, cooked, drained

Grated parmesan cheese

• In a roaster pan, over medium heat,
cook sausage as directed on package or
until browned and no longer pink,
stirring to separate meat.

• Stir in spaghetti sauce. Heat to boiling.

• Add ravioli. Heat through, stirring
occasionally.

• Pour into serving dish and sprinkle with
parmesan cheese.

Sausage Casserole

1 pound pork sausage

2 (15 ounce) cans pork and beans

1 (15 ounce) can Mexican style stewed tomatoes

1 package corn muffin mix

- Brown sausage and drain fat.
- Add beans and tomatoes and blend. Bring to a boil. Pour into a 3-quart greased casserole.
- Prepare muffin mix according to package. Drop by spoonfuls over meat and bean mixture.
- Bake at 400° for 30 minutes or until top is browned.

Tangy Pork Chops

4-6 pork chops

¼ cup worcestershire sauce

¼ cup ketchup

½ cup honey

- In skillet, brown pork chops. Place in a shallow baking dish.
- Combine worcestershire, ketchup and honey. Pour over pork chops.
- Cover and bake at 325° for 45 minutes.

Sweet & Sour Pork Chops

8 thick, boneless pork chops

⅓ cup soy sauce

⅓ cup chili sauce

½ cup honey

- Place pork chops in a shallow baking pan.
- Combine soy sauce, chili sauce and honey; pour over pork chops.
- Bake covered at 325° for 50 minutes.

Pork Chops Italiano

6 (½-inch thick) pork
chops

2 cups extra chunky
mushroom and green
pepper spaghetti sauce

1 (4 ounce) can sliced
mushrooms

Cooked rice

- In a large skillet in a little oil, brown the pork chops on both sides. Remove from skillet and set aside. Pour off fat.
- In the same skillet heat the spaghetti sauce and mushrooms.
- Return pork chops to skillet. Reduce heat to low.
- Cover and cook for another 25 minutes, stirring occasionally.

Serve over hot cooked rice.

Pork Chops and Apples

6 thick pork chops

Flour

Oil

3 baking apples

- Dip pork chops in flour and coat well. In a skillet, brown pork chops in oil. Place in a 9 x 13-inch greased casserole.
- Add about ⅓ cup water to casserole. Cook, covered at 325° for about 50 minutes.
- Peel, half and seed apples. Place ½ apple on top of each pork chop. Return to oven for about 10 minutes. (Don't overcook apples.)

Shrimp Newburg

1 (10½ ounce) can
condensed cream of
shrimp soup

¼ cup water

1 teaspoon seafood
seasoning

1 (1 pound) package
frozen cooked salad
shrimp, thawed

• In a saucepan, combine soup, water
and seafood seasoning. Bring to a boil.

• Reduce heat and stir in shrimp. Heat
thoroughly.

Serve over hot white rice.

Shrimp Scampi

1 pound shrimp, peeled
and deveined

1 teaspoons garlic salt

2 tablespoons lemon
juice

2 tablespoons butter

• Place shrimp in a shallow baking pan.

• Sprinkle with garlic salt and lemon
juice; dot with butter.

• Broil on one side for 3 minutes. Turn
and broil 3 minutes more.

Skillet Shrimp Scampi

2 teaspoons olive oil

2 pounds uncooked
shrimp, peeled and
deveined

⅔ cup herb and garlic
marinade with lemon
juice

¼ cup finely chopped
green onion and tops

• In large nonstick skillet, heat oil. Add
shrimp and marinade.

• Cook, stirring often until shrimp turns
pink. Stir in green onions.

*Serve over hot, cooked rice or your
favorite pasta.*

Italian Shrimp

2 sticks margarine

1 (8 ounce) bottle Italian dressing

⅓ cup lemon juice

3 pounds raw shrimp, peeled, deveined

- Melt margarine and mix dressing and lemon juice in skillet.
- Stir in shrimp. Saute for 10 to 15 minutes, turning occasionally.

Serve over rice.

Boiled Shrimp

3 pounds fresh shrimp

1 teaspoon salt

2 teaspoons seafood seasoning

½ cup vinegar

- Remove heads from shrimp.
- Place shrimp, salt, seasoning and vinegar in large saucepan. Cover shrimp with water and bring to boil.
- Reduce heat and boil for 10 minutes. Remove from heat and drain. Chill in refrigerator.

Creamed Shrimp Over Rice

3 cans frozen cream of shrimp soup

1 pint sour cream

1½ teaspoon curry powder

2 (5 ounce) cans deveined shrimp

- Combine all ingredients in top of double boiler.
- Heat, stirring constantly, but do not boil.

Serve over hot, cooked rice.

Crabmeat Casserole

2 (6 ounce) cans
  crabmeat, drained,
  picked

1 can french-fried onions,
  divided

1 (10½ ounce) can cream
  of chicken soup

¾ cup cracker crumbs

- In a bowl combine crabmeat, half of the fried onions, soup and cracker crumbs.
- Mix well and place in buttered casserole dish.
- Top with remaining french-fried onions.
- Bake covered at 350° for 30 minutes.

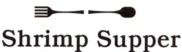

Shrimp Supper

1½ pounds cooked and
  peeled shrimp

1 small head lettuce,
  chopped

1 (14 ounce) jar
  artichokes, quartered,
  drained

1 avocado, sliced

- Combine all ingredients and serve with a creamy ranch dressing.

Seafood Casserole

1 (6 ounce) can crabmeat,
  drained, picked

1 (6 ounce) can shrimp,
  drained

1½ cup cracker crumbs,
  divided

1 (10½ ounce) can fiesta
  nacho cheese

- Combine crabmeat, shrimp, ¾ cup cracker crumbs and nacho cheese; mixing well.
- Place in a greased 1-quart baking dish. Sprinkle remaining crumbs on top.
- Bake uncovered at 350° for 30 minutes or until crumbs are lightly browned.

Curried Red Snapper

1½ pounds fresh red snapper

2 medium onions, chopped

2 celery ribs, chopped

1 teaspoon curry powder

¼ cup milk

- Place snapper in a greased 9 x 13-inch baking pan.
- In skillet, saute onions and celery in a little margarine. Add curry powder and a little salt; mixing well.
- Remove from heat; stir in milk. Spoon over snapper.
- Bake, uncovered at 350° for 25 minutes or until fish flakes easily with a fork.

Tuna and Chips

1 (6 ounce) can tuna, drained

1 (10½ ounce) can cream of chicken soup

¾ cup milk

1½ cups crushed potato chips, divided

- Break chunks of tuna into a bowl. Stir in soup and milk.
- Add ¾ cups crushed potato chips. Mix well.
- Pour into greased baking dish. Sprinkle the remaining chips over top.
- Bake uncovered at 350° for about 30 minutes or until chips are lightly brown.

Tuna Toast

1 (10½ ounce) can cream of chicken soup

1 (6 ounce) can tuna in water, drained

2 slices thick Texas toast

1 tomato, cut into chunks

- In saucepan, combine soup and tuna; stirring to break up chunks of tuna.
- Toast the Texas toast on both sides.
- Pour soup mixture over toast.
- Sprinkle tomatoes over soup mixture. Serve immediately.

Tuna Noodles

1 (8 ounce) package wide noodles, cooked, drained

2 (6 ounce) cans white tuna, drained

1 can cream of chicken soup, ¾ cup milk

¾ cup chopped black olives

- Place half the noodles in a 2-quart buttered casserole.
- In saucepan, combine the tuna, soup, milk and olives. Heat just enough to mix well.
- Pour half the soup mixture over noodles. Repeat layers.
- Cover and bake at 300° for about 20 minutes.

Home Fried Fish

1½ pounds haddock, sole or cod

1 egg beaten

2 tablespoons milk

2 cups corn flake crumbs

- Cut fish into serving-size pieces.
- Combine egg and milk. Dip fish in egg mixture and coat with the crushed corn flakes on both sides.
- Fry in a thin layer of oil in a skillet until brown on both sides.

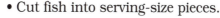

Crispy Flounder

⅓ cup mayonnaise

1 pound flounder fillets

1 cup seasoned breadcrumbs

¼ cup grated parmesan cheese

- Place mayonnaise in a small dish. Coat the fish with mayonnaise and dip in crumbs to coat well.
- Arrange in a shallow baking dish. Bake uncovered at 375° for 25 minutes.

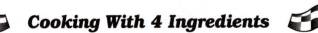
Haddock Fillets

1½ cups lemon lime soda

1 pound haddock fillets

2 cups pancake mix

¼ teaspoon pepper

• Pour soda in a shallow bowl; add fillets and let marinate for 15 minutes.

• In another shallow bowl combine pancake mix and pepper.

• Remove fish from soda and coat with pancake mix.

• In a large skillet heat about ¼-inch of oil. Fry fish for about 3 minutes on each side until fish flakes with a fork. Drain on paper towels.

Chipper Fish

2 pounds sole or orange roughy

½ cup Caesar salad dressing

1 cup crushed potato chips

½ cup shredded cheddar cheese

• Dip fish in dressing. Place in a greased baking dish.

• Combine chips and cheese; sprinkle over fish.

• Bake at 325° for about 20 minutes.

Red Fish Barbecue

2 pounds red fish fillets

1 (8 ounce) bottle Italian dressing

1 (12 ounce) can beer

Several dashes of Tabasco

• Place fish in a glass casserole dish. Pour Italian dressing, beer and Tabasco over fish.

• Cover and marinate in refrigerator at least two hours.

• When ready to cook, drain the fish and place in a microwave safe container.

• Microwave fish about 4 to 5 minutes per pound.

Crispy Fish Cheese Fillets

2 pounds fish fillets
½ cups creamy ranch-style dressing
1½ cups crushed cheese crackers
2 tablespoons margarine, melted

- Cut fish into serving portions. Dip into dressing and roll in cracker crumbs.
- Place on a greased shallow pan and drizzle margarine over fish.
- Bake uncovered at 425° for 15 minutes or until fish flakes easily.

Lemon Dill Fish

½ cup mayonnaise
2 tablespoons lemon juice
1 teaspoon dill weed
1 pound cod or flounder fillets

- Combine mayonnaise, lemon juice and dill until well blended.
- Place fish on greased grill or broiler rack. Brush with half of sauce.
- Grill or broil 5 to 8 minutes; turn and brush with remaining sauce.

Orange Roughy With Peppers

1½ pounds orange roughy
2 red bell peppers, cut into julienne strips
1 teaspoon dried thyme leaves
¾ teaspoon seasoned salt

- Cut fish into serving size pieces.
- Heat a little oil in a skillet. Layer the bell pepper and seasoning. Place fish on top.
- Turn burner on high until fish is hot enough to begin cooking.
- Lower heat, cover and cook fish for 15 to 20 minutes or until fish flakes easily.

Baked Halibut

2 pounds halibut steaks
(1 inch thick)

1 (8 ounce) carton sour
cream

½ cup grated parmesan
cheese

¾ teaspoon dill weed

• Place halibut in a greased 9 x 13-inch
baking dish.

• Combine the sour cream, parmesan
cheese and dill weed; salt and pepper if
desired. Spoon over halibut.

• Cover and bake at 325° for 20 minutes.

• Uncover and sprinkle with paprika.
Bake another 10 minutes longer or until
fish flakes easily with a fork.

Salmon Croquets

1 (15 ounce) can pink
salmon, drained, flaked

1 egg

½ cup biscuit mix

¼ cup ketchup

• Mix salmon (discarding skin and bones)
and egg in bowl.

• Add biscuit mix and ketchup; mix well.

• Heat a little oil in skillet and drop salmon
mixture by tablespoonfuls into skillet.

• Flatten each croquet with spatula. Cook
each side until brown.

Crab Potato Salad

5 potatoes, peeled and
cubed

2 (8 ounce) packages
imitation crabmeat,
chopped

1 cup finely chopped
onion

2 cups mayonnaise

• Place potatoes in a saucepan covered
with water; bring to a boil and cook for
about 20 minutes or until tender. Drain
and cool.

• In a large bowl combine the potatoes,
crab, onion, salt and pepper. Toss with
the mayonnaise.

• Refrigerate for about 3 hours before serving.

Baked Oysters

1 cup oysters, drained, rinsed

2 cups cracker crumbs

½ stick margarine, melted

½ cup milk

- Make alternate layers of oysters, cracker crumbs and margarine in a 7 x 11-inch baking dish.
- Pour warmed milk over layers adding lots of salt and pepper.
- Bake at 350° for about 35 minutes.

Butter Fish

Cod or flounder fillets

1 stick butter

Lemon juice

- Place butter in a shallow baking dish in a very hot oven until butter is melted and slightly browned.
- Place filets in hot butter and cook 10 minutes at 400°.
- Turn and baste with pan juices. Sprinkle fish with lemon juice and a little salt and pepper.
- Bake another 10 minutes or until fish flakes easily.

Salmon Patties

1 (15 ounce) can pink
   salmon, reserve juice

1 egg

1 teaspoon baking
   powder

½ cup cracker crumbs

- Pour off juice from salmon and set aside. Remove the bones and skin.
- Stir in egg and cracker crumbs with salmon.
- In a small bowl add baking powder to ¼ cup of salmon juice. Mixture will foam. After foaming add to salmon mixture.
- Drop by teaspoons in hot oil in skillet. Brown lightly on both sides. Serve hot.

DESSERTS

Caramel Cinnamon Dessert

1 (5 ounce) package
French vanilla instant
pudding

3 cups milk

1 (8 ounce) carton
whipped topping

1 box cinnamon graham
crackers

- Combine the pudding and milk, mixing well. Fold in whipped topping.
- Line bottom of a 9 x 13-inch glass dish with whole graham crackers.
- Put half the pudding mixture over crackers and top with a second layer of crackers. Spread remaining pudding over top. Top with the remaining crackers (you should have 2 or 3 crackers left over from the box).
- Add a prepared caramel icing over the last layer of graham crackers. Refrigerate.

  Make this a day ahead of time so the pudding can soak into the crackers.

Macaroon Delight

12 soft coconut
macaroons

1 (8 ounce) carton
whipping cream,
whipped

3 pints sherbet: 1 each,
orange, lime, raspberry,
softened

- Warm macaroons in a 300° oven for 10 minutes. Then break into pieces and cool.
- Spoon macaroons into the whipped cream.
- Completely line a 9 x 5-inch loaf pan with foil. First spread 1 pint of the orange sherbet in loaf pan.
- Then spread ½ of the whipped cream mixture, next the lime sherbet and the remaining whipped cream mixture. Raspberry sherbet will be on top.
- Freeze overnight. To serve unmold and remove foil and slice.

Caramel Apple Delight

3 (2.07 ounce) Snickers candy bars, frozen

2 Granny Smith apples, chopped

1 (12 ounce) carton whipped topping

1 (3 ounce) package dry instant vanilla pudding

- Smash frozen candy bars in the wrappers with a hammer.
- Mix all ingredients together.
- Refrigerate.

  Place in a pretty crystal bowl or serve in individual sherbet glasses.

Coffee Mallow

3 cups miniature marshmallows

½ cup hot, strong coffee

1 cup whipping cream, whipped

½ teaspoon vanilla

- In large saucepan, combine marshmallows and coffee. On low heat and stirring constantly, cook until marshmallows have melted. Cool this mixture.
- Fold in whipped cream and vanilla.
- Pour into individual dessert glasses. Stir until ready to serve.

Grape Fluff

1 cup grape juice

2 cups miniature marshmallows

2 tablespoons lemon juice

1 (8 ounce) carton whipping cream

- In saucepan heat grape juice to boiling. Add marshmallows. Stir constantly until melted.
- Add lemon juice and cool.
- Fold in whipped cream and spoon into individual serving dishes. Refrigerate.

Ice Cream Dessert

19 ice cream sandwiches

1 (12 ounce) carton
whipped topping,
thawed

1 (11¾ ounce) jar hot
fudge ice cream topping

1 cup salted peanuts

- Cut one ice cream sandwich in half. Place one whole and one half sandwich along a short side of an ungreased 9 x 13-inch pan. Arrange eight sandwiches in opposite direction in the pan.
- Spread with half of the whipped topping.
- Spoon fudge topping by teaspoonfuls onto whipped topping.
- Sprinkle with ½ cup peanuts.
- Repeat layers with remaining ice cream sandwiches, whipped topping and peanuts (pan will be full). Cover and freeze.

To serve, take out of freezer 20 minutes before serving.

Lemon Treat

1 (3 ounce) package
lemon pie filling mix
(not instant)

⅓ cup sugar

1 egg

½ (8 ounce) carton
whipped topping

- Mix pie filling, sugar and egg with ¼ cup water until smooth. Slowly add another 1¾ cup water.
- Cook, stirring constantly, over medium heat until mixture comes to a full boil. Remove from heat and cool completely.
- Fold in whipped topping and spoon into dessert dishes.

Top with a fresh strawberry or a slice of kiwi.

Apricot Pudding

1 (3.4 ounce) package vanilla pudding (not instant)

1 (15 ounce) can apricots, halved, reserve juice

1 (11 ounce) can mandarin oranges, drained

1 (8 ounce) carton whipped topping

• Cook pudding with 1¼ cups apricot juice (adding water to make the 1¼ cups). Cool.

• Add drained oranges and cut-up apricots. Refrigerate until mixture begins to thicken.

• Fold in whipped topping. Spoon into 6 individual sherbet dishes.

Peachy Sundaes

1 pint vanilla ice cream

¾ cup peach preserves, warmed

¼ cup chopped almonds, toasted

¼ cup coconut

• Divide ice cream into 4 sherbet dishes.

• Top with preserves.

• Sprinkle with almonds and coconut.

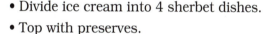

Mango Cream

2 soft mangoes

½ gallon vanilla ice cream, softened

1 (6 ounce) can frozen lemonade, thawed

1 (8 ounce) carton whipped topping

• Peel the mangoes and cut slices around the seed; then cut into small chunks.

• In a large bowl, mix together the ice cream, lemonade and whipped topping.

• Fold in the mango chunks.

• Quickly spoon mixture into parfait glasses or sherbets; cover with plastic wrap. Place in freezer.

Divinity Heaven

1 pint marshmallow
  cream

3 cups sugar

Pinch salt

⅔ cup chopped pecans

- Put marshmallow cream in a large bowl.
- In saucepan combine ½ cup water with sugar and salt. Bring to a rolling boil and boil exactly 2 minutes.
- Pour the sugar mixture into the marsh-mallow cream. Stir quickly.
- Add pecans and drop by teaspoonfuls onto wax paper.

Cookies and Cream

25 Oreo cookies, crushed

½ gallon vanilla ice
  cream, softened

1 (5 ounce) can chocolate
  syrup

1 (12 ounce) carton
  whipped topping

- Press crushed cookies in a 9 x 13-inch baking dish. Spread ice cream over cookies.
- Pour syrup over the ice cream and top with the whipped topping.
- Freeze overnight.
- Slice into squares to serve.

Peanut Butter Sundae

1 cup light corn syrup

1 cup chunky peanut
  butter

¼ cup milk

Ice cream or pound cake

- In a mixing bowl, stir together the corn syrup, peanut butter and milk until well blended.
- Serve over ice cream or pound cake. Store in refrigerator.

Strawberry Trifle

1 (5 ounce) package
French vanilla instant
pudding mix

1 (10 ounce) loaf pound
cake

½ cup sherry

2 cups fresh strawberries

- Make pudding as instructed on package.
- Place a layer of pound cake slices in the bottom of an 8-inch crystal bowl. Sprinkle with ¼ cup of the sherry. Add a layer of the strawberries. Next, add a layer of half the pudding. Repeat these layers. Refrigerate overnight or several hours.
- Before serving, top with whipped topping.

Amaretto Ice Cream

1 (8 ounce) carton
whipping cream,
whipped

1 pint vanilla ice cream,
softened

⅓ cup amaretto

⅓ cup chopped almonds,
toasted

- Combine whipped cream, ice cream and amaretto. Freeze in sherbet glasses.
- When ready to serve, drizzle a little additional amaretto over the top of each individual serving and sprinkle with toasted almonds.

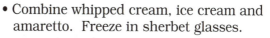

Blueberry Fluff

1 (20 ounce) can
blueberry pie filling

1 (20 ounce) can crushed
pineapple, drained

1 can sweetened,
condensed milk

1 (8 ounce) carton
whipped topping

- Mix pie filling, pineapple and condensed milk together.
- Fold in container of whipped topping. (This dessert is even better if you add ¾ cup of chopped pecans).
- Combine all ingredients and pour into parfait glasses. Refrigerate.

Winter Wonder Dessert

28 chocolate cream-filled chocolate cookies, divided

2¾ cup milk

3 (3.4 ounce) packages instant pistachio pudding

1 (8 ounce) carton whipped topping

- Crush the 28 cookies, reserving ⅔ of a cup. Place crushed cookies in a 9 x 13-inch dish.
- In mixing bowl, combine milk and instant pistachio pudding. Mix about 2 minutes until thickened. Pour over crushed cookies.
- Spread whipped topping over pistachio pudding.
- Sprinkle the reserved cookies over the top of whipped topping and refrigerate overnight before serving.

Divine Strawberries

1 quart fresh strawberries

1 (20 ounce) can pineapple chunks, well drained

2 bananas, sliced

2 (18 ounce) cartons strawberry glaze

- Cut strawberries in half (or in quarters if the strawberries are very large.)
- Add pineapple chunks and bananas.
- Fold in the strawberry glaze and chill.

This is wonderful served over pound cake or just served in sherbet glasses.

Amaretto Peaches

4½ cups peeled, sliced fresh peaches

½ cup amaretto

½ cup sour cream

½ cup packed brown sugar

• Lay the peaches in a 2-quart baking dish. Pour amaretto over peaches and spread sour cream over peaches. Sprinkle brown sugar evenly over all.

• Broil mixture until it is heated thoroughly and sugar melts.

Serve over ice cream or pound cake.

Brandied Apples

1 (10 ounce) loaf pound cake

1 (20 ounce) can apple pie filling

½ teaspoon allspice

2 tablespoons brandy

• Slice pound cake and place on dessert plates.

• In saucepan, combine pie filling, allspice and brandy. Heat and stir just until heated thoroughly.

• Place several spoonfuls over cake. Top with a scoop of vanilla ice cream.

Amaretto Sauce for Pound Cake

1 (3.4 ounce) package French vanilla pudding (not instant)

1 cup milk

1 (8 ounce) carton whipping cream, whipped

¼ cup amaretto

• Cook pudding with the milk according to package directions. Cover and cool to room temperature.

• With a wire whisk, stir in whipped cream and amaretto.

• Pour over pound cake or vanilla ice cream.

Boiled Custard

1 (14 ounce) can sweetened condensed milk

1 quart milk

4 eggs

½ teaspoon vanilla

- Combine the milk and heat in the top of a double boiler.
- In a separate pan, beat the eggs well.
- Slowly pour a little of the milk over the eggs, stirring constantly. Gradually add the eggs to the milk and cook on low for 5 to 10 minutes, stirring constantly, until thickened.
- Stir in vanilla and refrigerate.

  This can be served in custard cups or stemmed glasses.

Chocolate Coconut Mist

2 (14 ounce) packages flaked coconut

2 tablespoons butter, optional

1⅓ cups semi-sweet chocolate chips, melted

3 quarts mint chocolate chip ice cream

- In a bowl, toss coconut, butter (optional) and chocolate together until well blended.
- On a baking sheet covered with wax paper, shape about ⅓ cupfuls into 2⅓-inch nests. Chill until firm.

Just before serving top each nest with ½ cup of ice cream.

Brandied Apple Topping

1 (20 ounce) can apple pie
filling

¼ teaspoon allspice

¼ teaspoon cinnamon

4½ tablespoons brandy

• Pour apple pie filling on a dinner plate
or shallow bowl and cut apple slices into
smaller chunks. Place pie filling, allspice, cinnamon and brandy in a saucepan.

• Cook over medium heat for about 5
minutes.

• Pour topping over pound cake or vanilla
ice cream.

Black Forest Cake

1 devil's food cake mix

1 (20 ounce) can cherry
  pie filling

1 (3.4 ounce) package
  vanilla instant pudding

1 (8 ounce) whipped
  topping

• Bake cake according to directions in a greased and floured 9 x 13-inch baking pan.

• While cake is still warm poke top with fork and spread cherry pie filling over cake.

• While cake cools, prepare the pudding using 1 cup of milk. Fold in the whipped topping.

• Spread pudding and whipped topping mixture over cake, carefully covering the cherry pie filling. Refrigerate.

Pecan Cake

1 butter pecan cake mix

1 stick margarine, melted

1 egg

1 cup chopped pecans

• Combine cake mix, ¾ cup water, margarine and egg, mixing well. Stir in pecans.

• Pour into a 9 x 13-inch baking dish.

Topping for Pecan Cake:

1 (8 ounce) package
  cream cheese, softened

2 eggs

1 (1 pound) box powdered
  sugar

• With mixer, combine cream cheese, eggs and powdered sugar. Pour over cake mixture.

• Bake at 350° for 40 minutes. Check with toothpick to make sure cake is done.

Oreo Cake

1 package white cake mix
⅓ cup oil
4 egg whites
1¼ cups coarsely
 chopped Oreo cookies

• In a mixer bowl combine cake mix, oil, 1¼ cup water and egg whites. Blend on low speed until moistened. Then beat two minutes at high speed.

• Gently fold in coarsely chopped cookies. Pour batter into two greased and floured 8-inch round cake pans.

• Bake at 350° for 25 to 30 minutes or until toothpick inserted in center comes out clean.

• Cool for 15 minutes; then remove from pan. Let cool completely and frost.

Frosting for Oreo Cake

4¼ cups powdered sugar
2 sticks butter, softened
1 cup shortening (not
 butter flavored)
1 teaspoon almond
 flavoring

• With mixer combine all ingredients. Beat together until creamy.

• Ice the first layer of cake and place second layer on top; ice top and sides.

• Sprinkle with extra crushed Oreo cookies on top.

Favorite Cake

1 butter pecan cake mix
1 cup almond toffee bits
1 cup chopped pecans
Powdered sugar

• Mix cake mix according to package directions. Fold in toffee bits and pecans.

• Pour into a greased and floured bundt cake pan. Bake at 350° for 45 minutes or until toothpick inserted in center comes out clean.

• Allow cake to cool several minutes; then remove cake from pan. Dust with sifted powdered sugar.

Delightful Pear Cake

1 (15 ounce) can pears in light syrup, undrained

1 white cake mix

2 egg whites

1 egg

- Drain pears, reserving the liquid; chop pears.
- Place pears and the liquid in a mixing bowl; add cake mix, egg whites and egg. Beat on low speed for 30 seconds. Beat on high for 4 minutes.
- Grease and flour a 10-inch bundt pan. Pour in batter.
- Bake at 350° for 50 to 55 minutes. Cook until a toothpick inserted in middle comes out clean. Cool in pan for about 10 minutes. Remove cake and dust with sifted powdered sugar.

Miracle Cake

1 lemon cake mix

3 eggs

⅓ cup oil

1 (20 ounce) can crushed pineapple, undrained

- In mixing bowl combine all ingredients.
- Blend on low speed; then beat on medium for 2 minutes.
- Pour batter into a greased and floured 9 x 13-inch baking dish.
- Bake for 30 to 35 minutes until cake tests done with a toothpick.

Miracle Cake Topping

1 (14 ounce) can sweetened condensed milk

¼ cup lemon juice

1 (8 ounce) carton whipped topping

- Blend all ingredients, mixing well. Spread over cake. Refrigerate.

Chocolate Pudding Cake

1 milk chocolate cake
  mix

1¼ cups milk

⅓ cup oil

3 eggs

- In mixing bowl combine all ingredients. Beat well.
- Pour into a greased and buttered 9 x 13-inch baking pan.
- Bake at 350° for 35 minutes or cake tester comes out clean.

Frosting for Chocolate Pudding Cake

1 can sweetened
  condensed milk

¾ (16 ounce) can
  chocolate syrup

1 (8 ounce) carton
  whipped topping,
  thawed

⅓ cup chopped pecans

- In a small bowl mix the sweetened condensed milk and chocolate syrup.
- Pour over cake and let soak into cake. Chill for several hours.
- Spread whipped topping over top of cake and sprinkle pecans over the top. Refrigerate.

O'Shaughnessy's Special

1 (10 ounce) pound cake
  loaf

1 (15 ounce) can crushed
  pineapple, undrained

1 (3.4 ounce) box
  pistachio pudding mix

1 (8 ounce) carton
  whipped topping

- Slice cake horizontally, making 3 layers.
- Combine pineapple and pudding; beat until mixture begins to thicken; fold in whipped topping, blending well. (You may add a few drops of green food coloring if you would like the cake to be a brighter green).
- Spread on each layer and on top. Refrigerate.

Carnival Cake

1 white cake mix

2 (10 ounce) frozen sweetened strawberries, undrained

1 (3.4 ounce) package instant vanilla pudding

1 (8 ounce) carton whipped topping

- Make cake mix by following directions on box. Pour into a greased 9 x 13-inch baking dish. Bake according to package directions.

- When cool, poke holes with a knife in the top of the cake and pour strawberries over the top of the cake.

- Make up the package of instant pudding using 1¼ cups milk and when that is set, pour over the strawberries. Cover cake with the whipped topping. Refrigerate.

Apple Cake

1 box spiced cake mix

1 (20 ounce) can apple pie filling

2 eggs

⅓ cup chopped walnuts

- Combine all ingredients; mix very thoroughly with a spoon. Make sure all lumps from the cake mix are broken up.

- Pour into a greased and floured bundt pan.

- Bake at 350° for 50 minutes. Check with toothpick for doneness.

You may substitute any other pie filling for this cake.

Pineapple Angel Cake

1 (1-step) angel food cake mix

1 (20 ounce) can crushed pineapple, undrained

- Place angel food cake mix in mixing bowl and add pineapple and juice. Beat as directed on cake mix box.

- Pour into an ungreased 9 x 13-inch baking pan. Bake at 350° for 30 minutes.

This is a good low calorie cake.

Chocolate Cherry Cake

1 milk chocolate cake mix

1 (20 ounce) can cherry pie filling

3 eggs

- In mixing bowl, combine all ingredients. Mix by hand.
- Pour into a greased and floured 9 x 13-inch baking dish.
- Bake at 350° for 35 to 40 minutes. Test with toothpick for doneness.

Chocolate Cherry Cake Frosting

5 tablespoons margarine

1¼ cups sugar

½ cup milk

1 (6 ounce) package chocolate chips

- When cake is done, combine margarine, sugar and milk in a medium saucepan. Boil one minute, stirring constantly. Add chocolate chips and stir until chips are melted. Pour over hot cake.

Pink Lady Cake

1 strawberry cake mix

3 eggs

1 teaspoon lemon extract

1 (20 ounce) can strawberry pie filling

- In mixer, beat the cake mix, eggs and lemon extract together.
- Fold in pie filling.
- Pour in a greased and floured 9 x 13-baking pan.
- Bake at 350° for 30 to 35 minutes. Test with a toothpick to make sure that cake is done.

Add a prepared vanilla icing or whipped topping.

Hawaiian Dream Cake

1 yellow cake mix

4 eggs

¾ cup oil

½ (20 ounce) can crushed
pineapple with ½ juice

- With mixer beat together all ingredients for 4 minutes.
- Pour into a greased and floured 9 x 13-inch baking pan.
- Bake at 350° for 30 to 35 minutes or until cake tests done with toothpick. Cool.

Hawaiian Dream Cake
Coconut Pineapple Icing

½ (20 ounce) can crushed
pineapple with ½ juice

1 stick margarine

1 (16 ounce) box
powdered sugar

1 (7 ounce) can coconut

- Heat together the pineapple and margarine. Boil 1½ minutes.
- Add powdered sugar and coconut.
- Punch holes in cake with knife. Pour hot icing over cake.

Pound Cake Deluxe

1 (10 inch) round bakery
pound cake

1 (20 ounce) can crushed
pineapple, undrained

1 (5.1 ounce) package
coconut instant
pudding mix

1 (8 ounce) carton
whipped topping

- Slice cake horizontally to make 3 layers.
- Mix pineapple, pudding and whipped topping together, blending well.
- Spread on each layer and top of cake. Coconut can be sprinkled on top layer. Refrigerate.

Coconut Angel Cake

1 (14 ounce) 10-inch round angel food cake

1 (20 ounce) can coconut pie filling

1 (12 ounce) carton whipped topping

3 tablespoons coconut

- Cut angel food cake horizontally to make three layers.
- Combine coconut pie filling and whipped topping. Spread ⅓ of mixture on the first layer. Top with second layer.
- Spread ⅓ of mixture on the second layer and top with the third layer. Spread remaining whipped topping mixture on top of cake.
- Sprinkle the coconut on top of mixture. Refrigerate.

Fluffy Orange Cake

1 orange cake mix

4 eggs

⅔ cup oil

½ cup water

- In mixer bowl, combine all ingredients.
- Beat on low speed to blend then beat on medium speed for 2 minutes. Pour into a greased and floured 9 x 13-inch baking pan.
- Bake at 350° for 30 minutes or until cake tests done. Cool.

Topping for Fluffy Orange Cake

1 (14 ounce) can sweetened condensed milk

⅓ cup lemon juice

1 (8 ounce) carton whipped topping

2 (11 ounce) cans mandarin oranges, drained, cut in half, chilled

- In a large bowl blend condensed milk and lemon juice mixing well.
- Fold in whipped topping until blended. Fold in orange slices.
- Pour mixture over cooled cake. Cover and refrigerate.

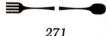

Basic Pound Cake

3 sticks of butter
3 cups sugar
8 eggs
3 cups sifted flour

- In mixer, cream together butter and sugar, mixing well.
- Add eggs one at a time, beating well after each addition. Add flour stirring in small amounts at a time.
- Pour into a greased and floured 10-inch bundt pan and bake at 300° for 1½ hours.

  Do not open oven door during baking.

Emergency Cheesecake

1 (8 ounce) package
  cream cheese, softened
1 can sweetened
  condensed milk
½ cup lemon juice
1 teaspoon vanilla

- Blend all ingredients in mixer.
- Pour into a graham cracker crust. Refrigerate.

  To serve, top with cherry pie filling.

Chiffon Torte

1 round bakery orange
  chiffon cake
1 (20 ounce) can crushed
  pineapple, undrained
1 (5.1 ounce) package
  vanilla instant pudding
1 (8 ounce) carton
  whipped topping

- Slice cake horizontally to make 3 layers.
- In mixer combine pineapple and pudding, beat by hand until mixture begins to thicken. Fold in whipped topping.
- Spread on each layer and cover top of cake.
- Refrigerate overnight.

  Toasted almonds can be sprinkled on top of cake.

Lemon Pineapple Cake

1 lemon cake mix

1 (20 ounce) can crushed pineapple, undrained

3 eggs

⅓ cup oil

- In mixing bowl, combine all ingredients. Blend on low speed to moisten, then beat on medium for 2 minutes.
- Pour batter into a greased and floured 9 x 13-inch baking pan.
- Bake at 350° for 30 minutes. Test with toothpick to be sure cake is done. When cake is baking start making the topping for the cake. Cool for about 15 minutes.

Topping for Moist Lemon Cake

1 (14 ounce) can sweetened condensed milk

1 cup sour cream

¼ cup lemon juice

- In medium bowl, combine all ingredients. Stir well to blend.
- Pour over warm cake. Refrigerate.

Chocolate Orange Cake

1 (16 ounce) loaf frozen pound cake, thawed

1 (12 ounce) jar orange marmalade

1 (16 ounce) can ready-to-spread chocolate fudge frosting

- Cut cake horizontally to make 3 layers.
- Place one layer on cake platter. Spread with ½ of the marmalade.
- Place second layer over first and spread on remaining marmalade.
- Top with third cake layer and spread frosting liberally on top and sides of cake. Refrigerate.

Easy Pineapple Cake

2 cups sugar

2 cups flour

1 (20 ounce) can crushed pineapple, undrained

1 teaspoon baking soda

- Combine all cake ingredients and mix by hand.
- Pour into a greased and floured 9 x 13-inch baking pan.
- Bake at 350° for 30 to 35 minutes.

Icing for Easy Pineapple Cake

1 (8 ounce) package cream cheese, softened

1 stick margarine, melted

1 cup powdered sugar

1 cup chopped pecans

- Combine cream cheese, margarine and powdered sugar and beat with mixer.
- Add the chopped pecans and pour over HOT cake.

Strawberry Delight

1 (6 ounce) package strawberry gelatin

2 (10 ounce) packages frozen strawberries, undrained

1 (8 ounce) carton whipped topping

1 (12 ounce) prepared angel food cake

- Dissolve strawberry gelatin in 1 cup boiling water; mixing well. Add strawberries.
- Chill in refrigerator until partially set.
- Fold in whipped topping.
- Break the angel food cake into large bite-size pieces and layer the cake and gelatin mixture ½ at a time in a 9 x 13-inch shallow dish. Refrigerate.

Cut in squares to serve.

Fruit Cocktail Cake

2 cups sugar
2 cups flour
1 teaspoon baking soda
2 (15 ounce) cans fruit cocktail, divided

- In mixer, combine sugar, flour, baking soda, 1 can fruit cocktail with juice and ½ of the other can fruit cocktail, but drain this can. (Reserve the ½ can fruit cocktail.)
- Beat several minutes with the mixer (fruit will be chopped up).
- Pour into a greased and floured 9 x 13-inch baking pan.
- Bake at 350° for 30 to 33 minutes. Test with toothpick to make sure cake is done. While cake is cooking, begin making icing to pour over hot cake.

Fruit Cocktail Cake Icing

1 (8 ounce) package cream cheese
1 stick margarine, softened
½ cup flaked coconut
1 (16 ounce) box powdered sugar

- Beat cream cheese and margarine together until creamy.
- Add remaining fruit cocktail, coconut and powdered sugar. Beat several minutes until fruit is chopped up.
- Pour over hot cake. When cool, store in refrigerator.

Pecans can be substituted for coconut.

Chocolate Amaretto Pie

2 (7 ounce) milk chocolate almond candy bars

⅓ cup amaretto

2 (8 ounce) cartons whipping cream, whipped

1 (9-inch) shortbread pie crust

- Melt chocolate in double boiler on low heat. Remove from heat and pour in amaretto.
- Stir chocolate and amaretto for about 10 or 15 minutes until mixture is room temperature.
- Fold in whipped cream.
- Pour into pie crust. Chill several hours before serving.

Key Lime Pie

6 egg yolks

2 (14 ounce) cans sweetened condensed milk

1 (8 ounce) bottle lime juice from concentrate

1 (9-inch) graham cracker crust

- In a large mixing bowl, beat egg yolks with sweetened condensed milk.
- Stir in the lime juice and green coloring if you like. Pour into graham cracker crust.
- Bake at 350° for about 20 minutes.
- Chill. Top with whipped cream.

Frozen Lemonade Pie

½ gallon frozen yogurt, softened

1 (6 ounce) can frozen pink lemonade, undiluted

1 (9-inch) graham cracker pie crust

- In large bowl, combine frozen yogurt and frozen pink lemonade. Work quickly.
- Pile ice cream mixture in pie crust and freeze.

Pink Lemonade Pie

1 (6 ounce) concentrated
pink lemonade, frozen

1 can sweetened
condensed milk

1 (8 ounce) package
whipped topping

1 (9-inch) graham cracker
pie crust

• In bowl, combine lemonade and the milk; blending well. Fold in whipped topping.

• Pour into pie crust and refrigerate overnight.

Magic Cherry Pie

2 (6 ounce) cartons
cherry yogurt

1 (3 ounce) package dry
cherry gelatin

1 (8 ounce) carton
whipped topping,
thawed

1 shortbread pie crust

• In a bowl, combine the yogurt and dry gelatin, mixing well.

• Fold in the whipped topping and spoon into pie crust.

• Freeze. Take out of freezer 20 minutes before slicing.

You could also place a dab of cherry pie filling on top of pie which will make it even better.

Limeade Pie

1 (6 ounce) can frozen limeade concentrate, thawed

2 cups lowfat frozen yogurt, softened

1 (8 ounce) carton whipped topping, thawed

1 (7-inch) graham cookie crumb pie crust

- In a large bowl, combine limeade concentrate and yogurt, mixing well.
- Fold in whipped topping.
- Pour into pie crust. Freeze at least 4 hours or overnight.

Cool Chocolate Pie

22 large marshmallows

2 (8 ounce) milk chocolate almond candy bars

1 (8 ounce) carton whipped topping

½ cup chopped pecans

- In a double boiler, melt marshmallows and chocolate bars.
- Cool partially and fold in whipped topping and pecans.
- Pour into a prepared graham cracker pie crust.
- Refrigerate several hours before serving.

Strawberry Almond Pie

2 (10 ounce) packages frozen sweetened strawberries, thawed

24 large marshmallows

1 (8 ounce) carton whipped topping

¼ cup slivered almonds, chopped, toasted

- Drain strawberries, reserving juice.
- In a saucepan, heat the strawberry juice and slowly add marshmallows. Heat on low. Stir until marshmallows are melted. Cool in refrigerator. Fold in whipped topping and strawberries.
- Pour into a shortbread pie crust.
- Sprinkle chopped almonds over top of pie. Refrigerate several hours.

Strawberry Pie

1 (6 ounce) box
   strawberry gelatin
¾ cup boiling water
1 (8 ounce) carton
   whipped topping
2 (10 ounce) packages
   strawberries, drain one
   package

- In a bowl, combine gelatin and boiling water, mixing well. Let gelatin cool in the refrigerator until it begins to thicken. (Watch closely.)
- Drain one package of strawberries, fold in whipped topping and strawberries.
- Spoon into a graham cracker crust.
- Refrigerate several hours before serving.

Million Dollar Pie

24 Ritz crackers,
   crumbled
1 cup chopped pecans
4 egg whites (absolutely
   no yolks at all)
1 cup sugar

- Mix cracker crumbs with pecans.
- In a separate mixing bowl, beat egg whites until stiff; slowly add sugar while still mixing.
- Gently fold in the crumbs and pecan mixture into egg whites. Pour into a pie tin and bake at 350° for 20 minutes. Cool before serving.

Top with a dip of chocolate ice cream.

Very Berry Pie

1 (6 ounce) package
   strawberry gelatin
1 (15 ounce) can whole
   cranberry sauce
½ cup cranberry juice
2 cups whipped topping

- Dissolve gelatin in ¾ cup boiling water.
- Add cranberry sauce and juice. Place in refrigerator until it begins to thicken.
- Fold in whipped topping and pour into a 9-inch graham cracker crust.

Apricot Pie

2 (15 ounce) cans apricot halves, drained

1¼ cups sugar

¼ cup flour

1 (8 ounce) carton whipping cream

- Cut each apricot half in half and arrange evenly in an unbaked, 9-inch pie shell.
- Combine sugar and flour and sprinkle over apricots.
- Pour unwhipped cream over pie.
- Place 1-inch strips of foil over edge of pie crust to keep from browning too much. Bake at 325° for 1 hour 20 minutes.

  You might want to place the pie on a cookie sheet to catch any possible spillovers.

Caramel Ice Cream Pie

1 roll butterscotch cookies

½ gallon vanilla ice cream

1 (12 ounce) jar caramel sauce

- Bake cookies according to directions on package.
- When cookies have cooled, crumble and place in a 10-inch pie plate keeping out about ½ cup to use for topping.
- Place ice cream in a bowl to soften. Stir caramel sauce into the ice cream (do not mix completely) and spoon mixture into the pie plate.
- Sprinkle remaining crumbs over top of pie. Freeze.

Pineapple Fluff Pie

1 (20 ounce) can crushed pineapple, undrained

1 (3.4 ounce) package instant lemon pudding mix

1 (8 ounce) carton whipped topping

1 (9 inch) graham cracker crust

• In a bowl, combine the pineapple and pudding mix; beat until thickened.

• Fold in the whipped topping.

• Spoon into pie crust.

• Refrigerate several hours before serving.

Margarita Pie

1 (8 ounce) package cream cheese, softened

⅓ cup sugar

2 envelopes margarita mix

1 (8 ounce) carton whipped topping

• In mixer bowl, whip cream cheese until fluffy.

• Add the sugar and the margarita mix and beat until smooth.

• Fold in whipped topping, mixing well. Pour into a shortbread ready pie crust. Freeze.

• Set out of refrigerator for 5 or 10 minutes before serving.

Apricot Chiffon Pie

2 (6 ounce) cartons apricot-mango yogurt

1 (3 ounce) box apricot gelatin

1 (8 ounce) carton whipped topping

1 (6 ounce) prepared shortbread pie crust

• In a bowl, combine yogurt and gelatin, mixing well.

• Fold in whipped topping and spread in pie crust. Freeze.

• Take out of freezer 20 minutes before slicing.

Holiday Pie

1 (8 ounce) package
  cream cheese, softened
1 (14 ounce) can
  sweetened condensed
  milk
1 (3.4 ounce box) instant
  vanilla pudding mix
1½ cups whipped topping,
  thawed

- With mixer, beat cream cheese until smooth. Gradually add sweetened condensed milk and beat until smooth.
- Add ¾ cup water and the pudding mix; beat until smooth.
- Fold in whipped topping.
- Pour into a graham cracker pie crust. Top with crumbled holiday candies.

Peaches N' Cream Pie

Chocolate syrup
1 quart peach ice cream,
  softened
Fresh peach slices
¼ cup pecan halves

- Drizzle ½ cup chocolate syrup over the bottom of a prepared shortbread pie crust.
- Spoon ice cream over crust and freeze for 3 hours or until firm.
- When ready to serve, place peach slices and pecan halves over top of ice cream.
- Drizzle with additional chocolate syrup.

Sunny Lime Pie

2 (6 ounce) cartons key
  lime pie yogurt
1 (3 ounce) package dry
  lime gelatin
1 (8 ounce) carton
  whipped topping
1 (9-inch) graham cracker
  pie crust

- In a bowl, combine yogurt and lime gelatin; mixing well.
- Fold in whipped topping and spread in pie crust. Freeze.
- Take out of freezer 20 minutes before slicing.

Cheesecake Pie

1 (20 ounce) can
   strawberry pie filling,
   divided

2 cups milk

2 (3.4 serving size)
   packages instant
   cheesecake flavor
   pudding mix

½ (8 ounce) carton
   whipped topping,
   thawed

- Spoon ¾ cup pie filling into a graham cracker pie crust.
- In mixing bowl, combine milk and the pudding mixes. Beat for two minutes or until smooth. Mixture will be thick.
- Fold in whipped topping. Spoon over pie filling in crust.
- Refrigerate at least 3 hours. When ready to serve, top with remaining pie filling.

Banana Split Pie

3 small bananas

1 quart vanilla ice cream,
   softened

Fudge sauce, whipped
   topping

Chopped pecans,
   maraschino cherries

- Slice bananas and place on a graham cracker pie crust.
- Spoon softened ice cream over bananas. Freeze for 2 to 3 hours.
- Spread some fudge sauce over the ice cream and top with a layer of whipped topping.
- When ready to serve, place a maraschino cherry on top of each piece of pie.

Cookies N' Cream Pie

2 cups whole milk

2 (3.4 ounce) packages instant vanilla pudding mix

1 (8 ounce) carton whipped topping, thawed

1 cup crushed Oreo cookies

- In mixing bowl, combine milk and pudding mixes. Beat 1 minute or until well blended. Let stand for 5 minutes.
- Fold in whipped topping and crushed cookies. Spoon into a prepared chocolate pie crust.
- Refrigerate until firm.

Patrick's Pie

1 (8 ounce) package cream cheese, softened

Heaping ⅓ cup sugar

1 (8 ounce) carton whipped topping, thawed

1 cup chopped Fudge Shop grasshopper cookies

- With mixer, beat cream cheese and sugar together until well blended.
- Fold in whipped topping, mixing well.
- Add cookies and about 3 drops of green food coloring, if you like.
- Pour into a prepared chocolate pie crust. Garnish with extra crumbled cookies. Freeze.

Grasshopper Pie

22 large marshmallows

⅓ cup creme de menthe

1 (12 ounce) cartons whipping cream, whipped

1 (9-inch) prepared chocolate pie crust

- In a large saucepan, melt marshmallows with the creme de menthe over low heat. Cool.
- Fold the whipped cream into the marshmallow mixture.
- Pour filling into pie crust and freeze until ready to serve.

Peach Crunch

2 (20 ounce) cans peach
pie filling

1 white cake mix

1 cup slivered almonds

1 stick margarine

- Add pie filling evenly in the bottom of a greased and floured 9 x 13-inch baking pan.

- Sprinkle cake mix evenly and smooth over top. Sprinkle almonds evenly over cake mix.

- Slice butter into ⅛-inch slices and place over entire surface.

- Bake at 350° for 40 to 45 minutes or until top is nicely browned.

Blueberry Cobbler

2 (20 ounce) cans
blueberry pie filling

1 box white cake mix

1 egg

1 stick margarine,
softened

- Spread pie filling in a greased 9 x 13-inch baking dish.

- With mixer, combine cake mix, egg and margarine. Blend well. Mixture will be stiff.

- Spoon over filling.

- Bake at 350° for 45 minutes or until golden brown.

Cherry Cobbler

2 (20 ounce) cans cherry pie filling

1 package white cake mix

1½ sticks margarine, melted

1 (4 ounce) package slivered almonds

• Spread pie filling in a greased 9 x 13-inch baking pan.

• Sprinkle cake mix over the cherries.

• Drizzle melted margarine over top. Sprinkle almonds over the top.

• Bake at 350° for 45 minutes. Top with whipped topping.

Cream Cheese Crust

1 stick margarine, softened

1 (3 ounce) package cream cheese, softened

1 cup flour

• Combine margarine, cream cheese and flour.

• Blend with a pastry blender or with a fork until mixture can be made into a ball.

• Chill pastry for about one hour.

• Roll out on a floured surface.

Makes one 9-inch crust.

Cherry Crisp

2 (20 ounce) cans cherry pie filling

1 box white cake mix

1 stick margarine

2 cups chopped pecans

• Pour pie filling into a greased 9 x 13-inch baking dish.

• Sprinkle cake mix over top of filling.

• Dot with margarine and cover with pecans.

• Bake uncovered at 350° for 45 minutes.

Easy Pumpkin Pie

1 (9-inch) unbaked deep-dish pie shell

2 eggs

1 (30 ounce) can pumpkin pie mix

1 (5 ounce) can evaporated milk

• Beat eggs lightly in a large bowl. Stir in pumpkin pie mix and evaporated milk.

• Pour into pie shell.

• Cut 2-inch strips of foil and cover pie crust edges. This will keep pie crust from getting too brown.

• Bake at 400° for 15 minutes. Reduce temperature to 325° and bake for 40 more minutes or until knife inserted in center come out clean. Cool.

Butter Cookie Special

1 box butter cake mix

1 (3.4 ounce) package butterscotch instant pudding mix

1 cup oil, 1 egg, beaten

1¼ cups chopped pecans

- Mixing by hand stir together cake mix, pudding mix, oil and egg. Beat thoroughly.
- Stir in pecans. With a teaspoon place cookie dough on cookie sheet about 2 inches apart.
- Bake at 350° for about 8 minutes. Do not overcook.

Coconut Macaroons

2 (7 ounce) packages flaked coconut

1 (14 ounce) can Eagle brand condensed milk

2 teaspoons vanilla

½ teaspoon almond extract

- In a mixing bowl combine coconut, condensed milk and extracts; mix well.
- Drop by rounded teaspoons onto a foil lined cookie sheet.
- Bake at 350° for 8 to 10 minutes or until lightly browned around edges. Immediately remove from foil. (Macaroons will stick if allowed to cool). Store at room temperature.

Chocolate Crunch Cookies

1 package German chocolate cake mix with pudding

1 egg, slightly beaten

1 stick margarine, melted

1 cup crisp rice cereal

- Combine cake mix, egg and margarine. Add cereal; stir until blended.
- Shape dough into 1-inch balls. Place on lightly greased cookie sheet.
- Dip a fork in flour and flatten cookies in a crisscross pattern. Bake at 350° for 10 to 12 minutes. Cool.

Double Chocolate Cookies

6 egg whites

3 cups powdered sugar

¼ cup cocoa

3½ cups finely chopped pecans

- Beat egg whites until light and frothy. Fold sugar and cocoa into egg whites and beat lightly. Fold in pecans.
- Drop by teaspoons on a lightly greased and floured cookie sheet.
- Bake at 325° for about 20 minutes. Do not overbake and cool completely before removing from cookie sheet.

Lemon Cookies

1 stick butter, softened

1 cup sugar

2 tablespoons lemon juice

2 cups flour

- Cream butter, sugar and lemon juice slowly stirring in flour.
- Drop by teaspoons onto ungreased cookie sheet.
- Bake at 350° for 14 to 15 minutes.

Angel Macaroons

1 (16 ounce) package 1-step angel food cake mix

½ cup water

1½ teaspoons almond extract

2 cups flaked coconut

- With mixer, beat cake mix, water and extract on low speed for 30 seconds. Scrape bowl; beat on medium for 1 minute. Fold in coconut.
- Drop by rounded teaspoonfuls onto a parchment paper-lined baking sheet.
- Bake at 350° for 10 to 12 minutes or until set. Remove paper with cookies to a wire rack to cool.

Coconut Moments

2 sticks margarine, softened

½ cup powdered sugar

½ cup corn starch, 1 ⅓ cups flour

Flaked coconut

- Beat margarine and powdered sugar until light and fluffy. Add corn starch and flour; beat until well blended. Cover and refrigerate for one hour.
- Remove and shape into 1-inch balls. Roll in flaked coconut. Place on ungreased cookie sheet.
- Bake at 325° for 12 to 15 minutes. Watch closely and don't let the coconut burn. Cool 2 or 3 minutes before removing from pan.

Drop Cookies

2 sticks margarine, softened

¾ cup corn starch

⅓ cup powdered sugar

1 cup flour

- Mix together the margarine, corn starch, sugar and flour, mixing well.
- Drop on cookie sheet in small balls and flatten slightly.
- Bake at 350° for about 15 minutes; do not brown. When cool, ice.

Icing for Drop Cookies

1 (3 ounce) package cream cheese, softened

1 teaspoon vanilla

1 cup powdered sugar

- Blend all ingredients together, mixing well. Ice cookies.

Lemon Coolers

1 box lemon cake mix

1 egg

2 cups whipped topping

Powdered sugar

- Mix by hand the cake mix, egg and whipped topping; mixing well.
- Roll into small balls and roll in powdered sugar.
- Place on a greased cookie sheet and bake 350° for 8 to 10 minutes. Cool.

Cheesecake Cookies

1 cup butter, softened

2 (3 ounce) packages
  cream cheese, softened

2 cups sugar

2 cups flour

- Cream together the butter and cream cheese. Add sugar, beating until light and fluffy. Add flour, beating well.
- Drop by teaspoons onto cookie sheet and bake at 350° for 12 to 15 minutes or until edges are golden.

These are made even better if you add 1 cup of chopped pecans.

Gingerbread Cookies

1½ sticks margarine,
  softened

2 egg yolks

1 spice cake mix

1 teaspoon ginger

- In a large bowl combine margarine and egg yolks. Gradually blend in cake mix and ginger, mixing well.
- Roll out to a ⅛-inch thickness on a lightly floured surface. Using your gingerbread cookie cutter, cut out your cookies and place 2 inches apart on cookie sheet.
- Bake at 375° for about 8 minutes or until edges are slightly browned. Cool cookies before transferring cookies to a cookie bowl.

Devil's Cookies

1 package devil's food
   cake mix

½ cup oil

2 eggs

¾ cup chopped pecans,
   optional

- Combine the cake mix, oil and eggs in a mixer bowl; mixing well.
- Drop by teaspoons onto a non-stick cookie sheet.
- Bake at 350° for 10 to 12 minutes. Cool and remove to a wire rack.

Nutty Fudgies

1 package fudge cake mix

1 (8 ounce) carton sour
   cream

⅔ cup peanut butter
   chips

½ cup chopped peanuts

- Beat cake mix and sour cream until well blended and mixture is smooth. Stir in peanut butter chips and peanuts.
- Drop by teaspoonfuls onto a greased cookie sheet.
- Bake at 350° for 10 to 12 minutes. Remove from oven and cool.

Nutty Peanut Butter Cookies

2 cups biscuit mix

1 can sweetened
   condensed milk, plus 2
   tablespoons sugar

½ cup peanut butter

¼ cup chopped peanuts

- Combine biscuit mix, condensed milk, sugar and peanut butter, mixing well. Add peanuts.
- Drop by heaping tablespoons onto a cookie sheet.
- Bake at 350° for 8 to 10 minutes. These cookies do not need to brown.

Peanut Butter Cookies

1 cup sugar
¾ cup light corn syrup
1 (16 ounce) jar crunchy
  peanut butter
4½ cups chow mein
  noodles

- In a saucepan over medium heat bring sugar and corn syrup to a boil; stir in peanut butter.
- Remove from heat. Stir in noodles.
- Drop by spoonfuls onto wax paper and allow to cool.

Butter Cookies

1 pound butter (not
  margarine)
¾ cup brown sugar
¾ cup granulated sugar
4½ cups flour

- Cream butter and sugars together and slowly add flour, mixing well. Batter will be very thick.
- Roll into small balls and place on an ungreased cookie sheet.
- Bake at 350° for about 15 minutes until only slightly brown. Do not overbake.

Butterscotch Cookies

1 (12 ounce) and 1 (6
  ounce) package
  butterscotch chips
2¼ cups chow mein
  noodles
½ cup chopped walnuts
¼ cup coconut

- Melt butterscotch chips in double boiler. Add noodles, walnuts and coconut.
- Drop by tablespoonfuls onto wax paper.

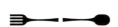

Pecan Puffs

2 egg whites
¾ cup packed light brown sugar
1 teaspoon vanilla
1 cup chopped pecans

- Beat egg whites until foamy. Gradually add (¼ cup at a time) brown sugar and vanilla. Continue beating until stiff peaks are formed (about 3 or 4 minutes). Fold in pecans.
- Line a cookie sheet with freezer paper.
- Drop by teaspoonfuls onto freezer paper.
- Bake at 250° for 45 minutes.

Scotch Shortbread

1 stick unsalted butter, softened
⅓ cup sugar
1¼ cups flour
Powdered sugar

- Cream butter and sugar until light and fluffy. Add flour and pinch of salt, mixing well.
- Spread dough in an 8-inch square pan.
- Bake at 325° for 20 minutes or until lightly brown.
- Let shortbread cool in pan and dust with powdered sugar and cut into squares.

Praline Grahams

1 package graham crackers (⅓ of a 16 ounce box)
¾ cup butter
½ cup sugar
1 cup chopped pecans

- Separate each graham cracker into four sections. Arrange in a jellyroll pan with edges touching.
- Melt butter in a saucepan; stir in sugar and pecans. Bring to a boil; cook 3 minutes, stirring frequently. Spread mixture evenly over graham crackers.
- Bake at 300° for 10 to 12 minutes. Remove from pan and cool on wax paper. Break up to serve.

Nutty Blonde Brownies

1 (1 pound) box light
  brown sugar

4 eggs

2 cups biscuit mix

2 cups chopped pecans

- In mixer, beat together the brown sugar, eggs and biscuit mix. Stir in pecans and pour into a greased 9 x 13-inch baking pan.

- Bake at 350° for 35 minutes. Cool and cut into squares.

Peanut Butter Brownies

1 (21 ounce) package
  brownie mix

1 cup peanut butter
  morsels

- Prepare brownie mix according to package directions, stirring in peanut butter morsels.

- Spoon mixture into a greased 9 x 13-inch baking pan.

- Bake at 350° for 35 minutes. Cool and cut into squares.

Peanut Butter Cups

1 (18 ounce) roll
  refrigerated peanut
  butter cookie dough

48 miniature peanut
  butter cup candy

- Slice cookie dough into ¾-inch slices. Cut each slice into quarters and place each quarter, pointed side up in a greased miniature muffin pan.

- Bake at 350° for 10 minutes.

- Remove from oven and immediately press a peanut butter cup candy gently and evenly into cookies. (Be sure you take paper wrapper off peanut butter cups). Cool and remove from pan and refrigerate until firm.

Chocolate Chip Cheese Bars

1 (18 ounce) tube refrigerated chocolate chip cookie dough

1 (8 ounce) package cream cheese, softened

½ cup sugar

1 egg

• Cut cookie dough in half. For crust, press half of the dough onto the bottom of a greased 9-inch square baking pan or a 7 x 11-inch baking pan.

• In a mixing bowl, beat cream cheese, sugar and egg until smooth. Spread over crust. Crumble remaining dough over top.

• Bake at 350° for 35 to 40 minutes or until a toothpick inserted near the center comes out clean. Cool on a wire rack. Cut into bars. Refrigerate leftovers.

Snicker Brownies

1 German chocolate cake mix

1½ sticks margarine, melted

½ cup evaporated milk

4 (2.7 ounce) snicker candy bars, sliced in ⅛-inch slices

• In a large bowl combine cake mix, margarine and evaporated milk. Beat on low speed until well blended.

• Add ½ of the batter into a greased and floured 9 x 13-inch baking pan.

• Bake at 350° for 10 minutes.

• Remove from oven and place candy bar slices evenly over the brownies. Drop remaining half of batter by spoonfuls over the candy bars; spread as evenly as possible.

• Place back in the oven and bake for 20 minutes longer. When cool cut into bars.

Walnut Bars

1⅔ cups graham cracker crumbs

1½ cups coarsely chopped walnuts

1 (14 ounce) can sweetened condensed milk

¼ cup coconut (optional)

- Place the graham cracker crumbs and walnuts in a bowl. Slowly add the condensed milk, coconut and a pinch of salt. Mixture will be very thick.
- Pack into a 9-inch square greased pan. Pack mixture down with the back of a spoon.
- Bake at 350° for 35 minutes. When cool cut into squares.

Apricot Bars

1¼ cups flour

¾ cup packed brown sugar

6 tablespoons margarine

¾ cup apricot preserves

- In mixing bowl, combine flour, brown sugar, and margarine, mixing well.
- Add ½ of this mixture into a 9-inch square baking pan. Spread the apricot preserves over top of mixture. Add remaining flour mixture over top of dessert.
- Bake at 350° for 30 minutes. Cut into squares.

Chocolate Drops

12 ounce package milk chocolate chips

⅔ cup chunky peanut butter

4¼ cups Cocoa Krispie cereal

- In double boiler, melt chocolate chips and stir in peanut butter. Stir in cereal.
- Press into a 9 x 9-inch pan. Cut into bars.

Chocolate Cherry Bars

1 devil's food cake mix

1 (20 ounce) can cherry pie filling

2 eggs

1 cup milk chocolate chips

• In a large bowl, mixing by hand combine all four ingredients, blending well.

• Pour batter into a greased and floured 9 x 13-inch baking dish.

• Bake at 350° for 25 to 30 minutes or until cake tester comes out clean. Cool and frost.

Frosting for Chocolate Cherry Bars

1 (3 ounce) square of semi-sweet chocolate, melted

1 (3 ounce) package cream cheese, softened

½ teaspoon vanilla

1½ cups powdered sugar

• In a medium bowl beat chocolate, cream cheese and vanilla until smooth. Gradually beat in powdered sugar.

• Pour over chocolate cherry bars.

Pecan Squares

1 (24 ounce) package almond bark

1 cup cinnamon chips

1 cup chopped pecans

8 cups frosted crispy rice cereal

• Melt almond bark and cinnamon chips in a very large saucepan or roaster on low heat, stirring constantly. When melted remove from heat and add pecans and frosted crispy rice cereal.

• Mix well and stir into a 9 x 13-inch pan. Pat down with the back of a spoon. Refrigerate just until set. Cut into squares.

Corn Flake Cookies

1 (12 ounce) package
butterscotch morsels

¾ cup peanut butter

3½ to 4 cups corn flakes,
crushed

• Melt butterscotch morsels on very low heat. Add peanut butter. When mixed thoroughly add corn flakes.

• Drop by teaspoons onto wax paper.

Butterscotch Crunchies

1 (12 ounce) package
butterscotch morsels

1¾ cups chow mein
noodles

1 cup chopped pecans

• Melt butterscotch morsels in heavy pan over a very low flame, stirring gently. Stir in noodles and pecans just until blended and coated.

• Drop mixture by teaspoonful onto wax paper. Refrigerate 30 minutes or until set.

Porcupine Clusters

¼ cup corn syrup

1 (12 ounce) package
white chocolate
morsels

2 cups chow mein
noodles

¾ cup salted peanuts

• On low heat, melt corn syrup and white chocolate chips. Pour over noodles and peanuts. Mixing well.

• Drop by teaspoon onto waxed paper.

• Refrigerate to harden. Store in airtight container.

Chocolate or butterscotch chips could be used instead of white chocolate morsels.

Tumbleweeds

1 (12 ounce) can salted
peanuts

1 (7 ounce) can potato
sticks, broken up

3 cups butterscotch chips

3 tablespoons peanut
butter

- Combine peanuts and potato sticks in a bowl; set aside.

- In microwave, heat butterscotch chips and peanut butter at 70% power for 1 to 2 minutes or until melted; stir every 30 seconds. Add to peanut mixture; stir to coat evenly.

- Drop by rounded tablespoonfuls onto waxed paper-lined baking sheet. Refrigerate until set, about 10 minutes.

Tiger Butter

1 pound white chocolate
or almond bark

½ cup chunky peanut
butter

1 cup semi-sweet
chocolate morsels

- Line a 15 x 10-inch jelly-roll pan with wax paper.

- Heat white chocolate in a microwave-safe bowl on high 1 to 2 minutes or until melted. Stir until smooth. Add peanut butter and microwave on high until melted. Stir again until smooth. Spread mixture evenly into prepared pan.

- In another microwave-safe bowl melt chocolate morsels on high until melted. Pour chocolate over peanut butter mixture and swirl through with a knife until you get desired effect. Refrigerate several hours until firm. Break into pieces.

Surprise Chocolates

2 pounds white chocolate (or almond bark)

2 cups Spanish peanuts

2 cups small pretzel sticks, broken

- Melt chocolate in a double boiler. Stir in peanuts and pretzels.
- Drop by teaspoonfuls onto wax paper. Work fast because mixture hardens quickly.
- Place in freezer for 1 hour before storing at room temperature.

Butterscotch Peanuts

1 (12 ounce) package butterscotch morsels

2 cups chow mein noodles

1 cup dry roasted peanuts

- In a saucepan, heat butterscotch morsels over low heat until completely melted. Add noodles and peanuts and stir until each piece is coated.
- Drop from spoon onto wax paper. Cool. Store in airtight container.

Marshmallow Treats

½ stick margarine

4 cups miniature marshmallows

½ cup chunky peanut butter

5 cups crispy rice cereal

- In saucepan, melt margarine and add marshmallows. Stir until melted and add peanut butter. Remove from heat. Add cereal, stirring well.
- Press mixture into a 9 x 13-inch pan. Cut in squares when cool.

Honey Nut Bars

⅓ cup margarine

¼ cup cocoa

1 (10 ounce) package miniature marshmallows

6 cups of Honey Nut Clusters cereal

- Melt margarine in a large saucepan and stir in the cocoa and marshmallows. Cook over low heat, stirring constantly until marshmallows are melted and mixture is smooth.
- Remove from heat and stir in honey nut clusters.
- Pour into a Pam sprayed 7 x 11-inch pan. With a spatula smooth mixture down in pan. Cool completely and cut into bars.

Raisin Crunch

¾ cup light corn syrup

1 cup sugar

1 cup crunchy peanut butter

1 (20 ounce) box raisin bran

- In saucepan combine corn syrup and sugar. Heat until sugar is thoroughly dissolved. Remove from heat and stir in peanut butter. Place raisin bran in a large container and pour sauce over the top. Mix in thoroughly.
- Pat mixture into a 9 x 13-inch pan and completely chill. Crunch can be cut into squares and stored in a airtight container.

Crazy Cocoa Crisps

24 ounces white almond bark

2¼ cups cocoa flavored crispy rice cereal

2 cups dry roasted peanuts

- Place almond bark in double boiler; heat and stir while bark is melting. Stir in cereal and peanuts.
- Drop by teaspoon on cookie sheet.
- Place in refrigerator for about 30 minutes to set. Store in airtight container.

Morning Meringues

2 egg whites, beaten stiff
3/4 cup sugar
1 cup nuts
1 cup chocolate chips

- Add sugar to stiffly beaten egg whites. Add in nuts and chocolate chips.
- Line a cookie sheet with foil. Drop by teaspoonfuls, pressing down.
- Bake at 350° for 10 minutes. Turn oven off. Let cookies sit in oven 8 to 10 hours.

Peanut Clusters

1 (24 ounce) package almond bark
1 (12 ounce) package milk chocolate chips
5 cups salted peanuts

- In double boiler, melt the almond bark and chocolate chips.
- Stir in peanuts and drop by teaspoons onto waxed paper.
- Place in refrigerator for 30 minutes to set. Store in airtight container.

Haystacks

1 (12 ounce) package butterscotch chips
1 cup salted peanuts
1½ cups chow mein noodles

- Melt butterscotch chips in the top of double boiler. Remove from heat and stir in peanuts and noodles.
- Drop by teaspoons on waxed paper. Cool and store in airtight container.

Peanutty Cocoa Puffs

¾ cup light corn syrup

1¼ cups sugar

1¼ cups chunky peanut butter

4½ cups cocoa puff cereal

- In a large saucepan bring syrup and sugar to a rolling boil. Stir in peanut butter; mixing well. Stir in cocoa puffs.
- Drop on wax paper by teaspoonful.

Caramel Apple Cupcakes

1 package carrot cake mix

3 cups chopped, peeled tart apples

1 (12 ounce) package butterscotch chips

1 cup finely chopped pecans

- Make cake batter according to package directions. Fold in apples. Fill 12 greased or paper lined jumbo muffin cups ¾ full.
- Bake at 350° for 20 minutes or until toothpick comes out clean.
- In a saucepan on very low heat melt the butterscotch chips. Spread over cupcakes and sprinkle with chopped pecans.

Scotch Crunchies

½ cup crunchy peanut butter

1 (6 ounce) package butterscotch bits

2½ cups frosted flakes

½ cup peanuts

- Combine peanut butter and butterscotch bits in a large saucepan; melt over low heat. Stir until butterscotch bits are melted. Stir in cereal and peanuts.
- Drop by teaspoonfuls onto wax paper. Refrigerate until firm. Store in air-tight container.

Peanut Butter Crunchies

1 cup sugar
½ cup white corn syrup
2 cups peanut butter
4 cups crispy rice cereal

- In a saucepan mix sugar and syrup and bring to a rolling boil. Remove from stove and stir in peanut butter. Add the crispy rice cereal, mixing well.
- Drop by the teaspoons onto wax paper. Place in refrigerator for a few minutes to set.

Pumpkin Cupcakes

1 (18 ounce) package spice cake mix
1 (15 ounce) can pumpkin
3 eggs
⅓ cup oil

- With mixer, blend cake mix, pumpkin, eggs, oil and ⅓ cup water. Beat for 2 minutes. Pour batter into 24 paper-lined muffin cups. Fill ¾ full.
- Bake at 350° for 18 to 20 minutes or until toothpick inserted in center comes out clean. You might want to spread with commercial icing.

Kid's Bars

1 cup each sugar and light corn syrup
1½ cups crunchy peanut butter
6 cups crispy rice cereal
1 (12 ounce) package chocolate chips

- In saucepan, combine sugar and corn syrup. Bring to a boil, stirring constantly. Remove from heat and stir in peanut butter and crispy rice cereal.
- Spread into a buttered 9 x 13-inch pan.
- In saucepan, over low heat, melt chocolate chips. Spread over cereal layer. Refrigerate until set; cut into bars. Store in refrigerator.

Tasty Treat

2 cups butterscotch
  morsels

2 cups salted peanuts

2 cups white raisins

• Mix all together and store in an airtight container.

Brown Sugar Cookies

¾ cup packed brown
  sugar

1 cup butter, softened

1 egg yolk

2 cups flour

• Cream sugar and butter until light and fluffy. Mix in egg yolk. Blend in flour. Refrigerate dough for 1 hour.

• Form dough into 1-inch balls, flatten and criss-cross with fork on lightly greased baking sheet.

• Bake at 325° for 10 to 12 minutes or until golden brown.

Macadamia Candy

2 (3 ounce) jars
Macadamia nuts
1 (20 ounce) package
white almond bark
¾ cup coconut

- Heat a dry skillet; toast nuts until slightly golden. (Some brands of Macadamias nuts are already toasted, so skip this step if they are.) Set aside.
- In a double boiler, melt the 12 squares of almond bark.
- As soon as almond bark is melted, pour the Macadamia nuts and coconut in. Stir well.
- Place a piece of waxed paper on a cookie sheet and pour the candy on the waxed paper; spread out. Refrigerate 30 minutes to set. Break into pieces.

Diamond Fudge

1 (6 ounce) package semi-sweet chocolate morsels
1 cup creamy peanut butter
1 stick margarine
1 cup powdered sugar

- Cook first 3 ingredients in a saucepan over low heat, stirring constantly, just until mixture melts and is smooth. Remove from heat.
- Add powdered sugar, stirring until smooth.
- Spoon into a buttered 8-inch square pan; chill until firm. Cut into squares.

Peanut Butter Fudge

12 ounces chunky peanut butter

12 ounces package milk chocolate chips

1 (14 ounce) can sweetened condensed milk

1 cup chopped pecans

- In saucepan, combine peanut butter, chocolate chips and condensed milk. Heat on low, stirring constantly until chocolate is melted.

- Add pecans, mixing well. Pour into a 9 x 9-inch buttered dish.

Raisin Fudge

1 (12 ounce) package semi-sweet chocolate chips

1 cup chunky peanut butter

3 cups miniature marshmallows

¾ cup raisins

- In a saucepan melt the chocolate chips and peanut butter over medium to low heat.

- Fold in the marshmallows and raisins; stir until marshmallows have melted. Pour into a 7 x 11-inch pan.

- Chill until firm. Cut into squares. Store where it is cool.

Microwave Fudge

3 cups semi-sweet chocolate morsels

1 (14 ounce) can sweetened condensed milk

½ stick margarine, cut into pieces

1 cup chopped walnuts

- Combine first 3 ingredients in a 2-quart glass bowl.

- Microwave at MEDIUM 4 to 5 minutes, stirring at 1½ minutes intervals.

- Stir in walnuts and pour into a buttered 8-inch square dish. Chill 2 hours. Cut into squares.

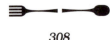

Dream Candy

2 (8 ounce) cartons whipping cream

3 cups sugar

1 cup light corn syrup

1 cup chopped pecans

- In a saucepan combine the whipping cream, sugar and corn syrup. Cook to a soft-boil stage.
- Stir and beat until candy is cool.
- Add pecans and pour into a 9-inch buttered pan.

Butterscotch Candy

1 (16 ounce) package butterscotch morsels

3 heaping tablespoons chunky peanut butter

1½ cups peanuts

1 can shoestring potatoes

- In a saucepan, on low heat, melt butterscotch morsels and peanut butter.
- Add peanuts and shoestring potatoes.
- Drop by the spoonfuls onto wax paper. Place in refrigerator until candy is set.

Chocolate Toffee

1 cup sugar

2 sticks butter

1 (6 ounce) package chocolate chips

1 cup chopped pecans

- In a heavy saucepan, combine sugar and butter. Cook until candy reaches a hard-crack stage. Pour onto a greased baking sheet.
- Melt chocolate in a double boiler and spread over toffee.
- Sprinkle with pecans; pressing pecans into the chocolate.
- Chill briefly to set chocolate. Break into pieces.

Fudge

1 (16 ounce) package
semi-sweet chocolate
chips

1 (14 ounce) can
sweetened condensed
milk

1 teaspoon vanilla

1 cup chopped pecans

- Melt chocolate chips in double boiler.
- Pour in the milk, vanilla and pecans and stir.
- Pour into a 9-inch buttered dish.
- Refrigerate until firm. Cut into squares to serve.

Date Loaf Candy

3 cups sugar

1 cup milk

1 (16 ounce) box chopped
dates

1 cup chopped pecans

- Combine sugar and milk in large saucepan.
- Cook to a soft-boil stage (234° on a candy thermometer). Stir in dates. Cook to a hard boil stage (260°), stirring constantly.
- Remove from heat; add pecans and mix well. Stir and cool until stiff. Pour mixture onto a damp tea towel.
- Roll into a log. Let stand until set. When candy is set, remove the tea towel and slice.

Pecan Topped Toffee

2 sticks butter (the real thing)

1¼ cups packed brown sugar

6 (1.5 ounce) milk chocolate bars

⅔ cup finely chopped pecans

• In saucepan combine the butter and sugar. Cook on medium high heat, stirring constantly until mixture reaches 300° on candy thermometer. Pour immediately into a greased 9-inch baking pan.

• Lay chocolate bars evenly over hot candy. When the candy is soft, spread into a smooth layer.

• Sprinkle pecans over the chocolate and press lightly with the back of your spoon. Chill in refrigerator for about one hour.

• Invert candy onto a piece of waxed paper and break into small irregular pieces.

Cooking With 4 Ingredients

Index

Index

Master Grocery List

FRESH PRODUCE

___ Apples
___ Avocados
___ Bananas
___ Beans
___ Bell Peppers
___ Broccoli
___ Cabbage
___ Carrots
___ Cauliflower
___ Celery
___ Corn
___ Cucumbers
___ Garlic
___ Grapefruit
___ Grapes
___ Lemons
___ Lettuce
___ Lime
___ Melons
___ Mushrooms
___ Onions
___ Oranges
___ Peaches
___ Pears
___ Peppers
___ Potatoes
___ Strawberries
___ Spinach
___ Squash
___ Tomatoes
___ Zucchini
___ _____
___ _____

FRESH BAKERY

___ Bagels
___ Bread
___ Cake
___ Cookies
___ Croissants
___ Donuts
___ French Bread
___ Muffins
___ Pastries
___ Pies
___ Rolls
___ _____
___ _____

DAIRY

___ Biscuits
___ Butter
___ Cheese
___ Cottage Cheese
___ Cream Cheese
___ Cream
___ Creamer
___ Eggs
___ Juice
___ Margarine
___ Milk
___ Pudding
___ Sour Cream
___ Yogurt
___ _____
___ _____

DELI

___ Cheese
___ Chicken
___ Main Dish
___ Prepared Salad
___ Sandwich Meat
___ Side Dishes
___ _____
___ _____

FROZEN FOODS

___ Breakfast
___ Dinners
___ Ice
___ Ice Cream
___ Juice
___ Pastries
___ Pies
___ Pizza
___ Potatoes
___ Vegetables
___ Whipped Cream
___ _____
___ _____

OTHER

___ _____
___ _____
___ _____
___ _____

Master Grocery List

GROCERY

___ Beans
___ Beer/Wine
___ Bread
___ Canned Vegetables
___ _____
___ _____
___ Cereal
___ Chips/Snacks
___ Coffee
___ Cookies
___ Crackers
___ Flour
___ Honey
___ Jelly
___ Juice
___ Ketchup
___ Kool-Aid
___ Mayonnaise
___ Mixes
___ _____
___ _____
___ Mustard
___ Nuts/Seeds
___ Oil
___ Pasta
___ Peanut Butter
___ Pickles/Olives
___ Popcorn
___ Rice
___ Salad Dressing
___ Salt
___ Seasonings
___ _____
___ _____

___ Sauce
___ Sodas
___ Soups
___ Spices
___ _____
___ _____
___ _____
___ Sugar
___ Syrup
___ Tea
___ Tortillas
___ Water
___ _____
___ _____
___ _____

MEAT

___ Bacon
___ Chicken
___ Ground Beef
___ Ham
___ Hot Dogs
___ Pork
___ Roast
___ Sandwich Meat
___ Sausage
___ Steak
___ Turkey
___ _____
___ _____
___ _____

GENERAL MERCHANDISE

___ Automotive
___ Baby Items
___ _____
___ _____
___ _____
___ Bath Soap
___ Bath Tissue
___ Deodorant
___ Detergent
___ Dish Soap
___ Facial Tissue
___ Feminine Products
___ Aluminum Foil
___ Greeting Cards
___ Hardware
___ Insecticides
___ Light Bulbs
___ Lotion
___ Medicine
___ Napkins
___ Paper Plates
___ Paper Towels
___ Pet Supplies
___ Prescriptions
___ Shampoo
___ Toothpaste
___ Vitamins
___ _____
___ _____
___ _____

Substitutions

Food	Amount	Substitution
Breadcrumbs, dry	1 cup	¾ cup cracker crumbs
Broth, chicken or beef	1 cup	1 bouillon cube; 1 teaspoon granules in 1 cup boiling water
Butter	1 cup (4 ounces)	⅞ cup vegetable oil or shortening; 1 cup margarine
Buttermilk	1 cup	1 tablespoon lemon juice or white vinegar plus milk to equal 1 cup (must stand for 5 minutes)
Cottage cheese	1 cup	1 cup ricotta
Cornstarch	1 tablespoon	2 tablespoons flour
Cream, whipping	1 cup	4 ounces frozen whipped topping
Flour	1 cup sifted all-purpose	1 cup minus 2 tablespoons unsifted all-purpose
	1 cup sifted self-rising	1 cup sifted all-purpose flour plus 1 ½ teaspoon baking powder plus ⅛ teaspoon salt
Garlic	1 small clove	⅛ teaspoon garlic powder
Herbs	1 tablespoon fresh	1 teaspoon dried
Honey	1 cup	1 ¼ cups granulated sugar plus ⅓ cup liquid in recipe
Ketchup	½ cup	½ cup tomato sauce plus 2 tablespoons sugar plus 1 tablespoon vinegar
Lemon juice	1 teaspoon	½ teaspoon vinegar
Mushrooms	½ pound fresh	1 (6 ounce) can, drained
Mustard	1 tablespoon prepared	1 teaspoon dried
Onions	1 small	1 tablespoon instant minced; ½ tablespoon onion powder
Sour cream	1 cup	1 cup plain yogurt; ¾ cup buttermilk; 1 tablespoon lemon juice plus enough evaporated milk to equal 1 cup
Sugar	1 cup light brown	½ cup packed brown sugar plus ½ cup granulated sugar
	1 cup granulated	1 ¾ cups confectioners sugar; 1 cup packed brown sugar; 1 cup superfine sugar
Tomato juice	1 cup	½ cup tomato sauce plus ½ cup water
Tomato sauce	1 cup	½ cup tomato paste plus ½ cup water
Yogurt	1 cup	1 cup buttermilk; 1 cup milk plus 1 tablespoon lemon juice

Pan Sizes

Pan Sizes	Approximate Volume
Muffin Pans	
1 ¾ x ¾ mini	⅛ cup (2 tablespoons)
2 ¾ x 1 ⅛	¼ cup
2 ¾ x 1 ⅜	Scant ½ cup
3 x 1 ¼ jumbo	⅝ cup
Loaf Pans	
5 ½ x 3 x 2 ½	2 cups
6 x 4 ½ x 3	3 cups
8 x 4 x 2 ½	4 cups
8 ½ x 4 ¼ x 3	5 cups
9 x 5 x 3	8 cups
Pie Pans	
7 x 1 ¼	2 cups
8 x 1 ¼	3 cups
8 x 1 ½	4 cups
9 x 1 ¼	4 cups
9 x 1 ½	5 cups
10 x 2	6 cups

Pan Sizes	Approximate Volume
Cake Pans	
5 x 2 round	2 ⅔ cups
6 x 2 round	3 ¾ cups
8 x 1 ½ round	4 cups
7 x 2 round	5 ¼ cups
8 x 2 round	6 cups
9 x 1 ½ round	6 cups
9 x 2 round	8 cups
9 x 3 bundt	9 cups
10 x 3 ½ bundt	12 cups
9 ½ x 2 ½ springform	10 cups
10 x 2 ½ springform	12 cups
8 x 3 tube	9 cups
9 x 4 tube	11 cups
10 x 4 tube	16 cups
Casseroles	
8 x 8 x 12 square	8 cups
11 x 7 x 2 rectangular	8 cups
9 x 9 x 2 square	10 cups
13 x 9 x 2 rectangular	15 cups
1-quart casserole	4 cups
2-quart casserole	8 cups
2 ½-quart casserole	10 cups
3-quart casserole	12 cups

U.S. Measurements

3 teaspoons	1 tablespoon	
4 tablespoons	¼ cup	2 fluid ounces
8 tablespoons	½ cup	4 fluid ounces
12 tablespoons	¾ cup	6 fluid ounces
16 tablespoons	1 cup	8 fluid ounces
¼ cup	4 tablespoons	2 fluid ounces
⅓ cup	5 tablespoons + 1 teaspoon	
½ cup	8 tablespoons	4 fluid ounces
⅔ cup	10 tablespoons + 2 teaspoons	
¾ cup	12 tablespoons	6 fluid ounces
1 cup	16 tablespoons	8 fluid ounces
1 cup	½ pint	
2 cups	1 pint	16 fluid ounces
3 cups	1 ½ pints	24 fluid ounces
4 cups	1 quart	32 fluid ounces
8 cups	2 quarts	64 fluid ounces
1 pint	2 cups	16 fluid ounces
2 pints	1 quart	
1 quart	2 pints; 4 cups	32 fluid ounces
4 quarts	1 gallon; 8 pints; 16 cups	
8 quarts	1 peck	
4 pecks	1 bushel	

COOKBOOKS PUBLISHED
BY COOKBOOK RESOURCES

Mother's Recipes

Recipe Keepsakes

Quick Fixes With Mixes

Cooking With 5 Ingredients

The New Cooking With 4 Ingredients

Kitchen Keepsakes & More Kitchen Keepsakes

Mealtimes and Memories

Best of Busy People's Cookbooks

Cookbook 25 Years

Texas Longhorn Cookbook

Holiday Treats

Homecoming

Cookin' With Will Rogers

Best of Lone Star Legacy Cookbook

Little Taste of Texas

Little Taste of Texas II

Southwest Sizzler

Southwest Ole

Class Favorites

Favorite Treats

Leaving Home

Simply Simpatico